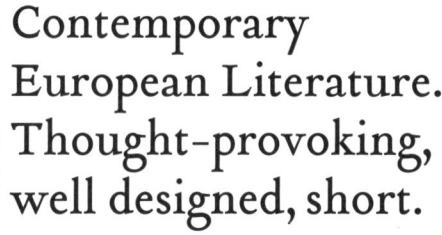

Contemporary European Literature. Thought-provoking, well designed, short.

Subscribe to Peirene and receive a beautiful book of world-class literature every four months delivered directly to your doorstep.

£35 1 year subscription (3 BOOKS, FREE UK P&P)
£65 2 year subscription (6 BOOKS, FREE UK P&P)
£90 3 year subscription (9 BOOKS, FREE UK P&P)

'Two-hour books to be devoured in a single sitting: literary cinema for those fatigued by film.' TLS

www.peirenepress.com

Follow us on Twitter and Facebook @PeirenePress

SPRING 2016 NEW TITLES

Beverley Bie Brahic, *Hunting the Boar*
978-1-909585-18-8; £8.99

David Collard, *About a Girl: A Reader's Guide to Eimear McBride's* A Girl Is a Half-formed Thing
978-1-909585-06-5; £12.00

Will Eaves, *The Inevitable Gift Shop*
978-1-909585-17-1; £8.99

Patrick Mackie, *The Further Adventures Of The Lives Of The Saints*
978-1-909585-14-0; £8.99

Jack Robinson, *by the same author*
978-1-909585-19-5; £5.00

Julian Stannard, *What were you thinking?*
978-1-909585-11-9; £8.99

CB editions

www.cbeditions.com

'exceedingly classy' – Patricia Duncker
'wonderfully eclectic, quietly iconoclastic' – Mike Loveday
'admirably wayward' – Jeremy Noel-Tod

Trade orders: Central Books
Representation: Inpress Books

free UK delivery for website orders

Sonofabook 2 edited by Sophie Lewis

Spring 2016

---

5   Editorial

8   **Adriana Lisboa** Two Poems
    trans. Alison Entrekin

13 **Emmanuelle Pagano** Two Stories
    trans. Jennifer Higgins

22 **Pierre Reverdy** *Au soleil du plafond* / Sun on the Ceiling
    trans. Dan Bellm

43 **Julián Herbert** Two Stories, One Poem
    trans. Lorna Scott Fox

51 **Taras Prokhasko** from *The Unsimple*
    trans. Uilleam Blacker

81 **Salim Barakat** from *The Caves of Hydrahodahose*
    trans. Sawad Hussein

97 **Luke Carman** A Portrait of the Artist in Residence

111 **Gabrielle Wittkop** from *Every Day Is a Tree that Falls*
    trans. Louise Rogers Lalaurie

123 **Pierre Senges** from *Geometry in the Dust*
    trans. Jacob Siefring

139 Contributors

Cover: *Puerto Azul* (1927) by Xul Solar (see page 142). Copyright Fundación Pan Klub-Museo Xul Solar, Buenos Aires, República Argentina.

Sonofabook is published by CB editions, 146 Percy Road, London W12 9QL. The contents of each issue are selected by a different editor. Copyright in each contribution remains with the author/translator. To subscribe, see www.cbeditions.com. Advertising: info@cbeditions.com. Distributed by Central Books; represented by Inpress Books. CB editions acknowledges the financial assistance of Arts Council England in the publication of this magazine. Printed in England by T. J. International, Padstow, Cornwall. ISBN 978-1-909585-16-4.

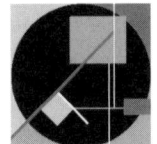

Five Leaves Bookshop

Nottingham's independent bookshop

The only UK city-centre independent bookshop to open this century

Cityscape and landscape, politics, fiction and poetry, lesbian and gay, psychology, weird and wonderful, international writing, counterculture, magazines and journals

14a Long Row, Nottingham NG1 2DH
10–5.30 Monday–Saturday
12–4 Sunday   0115 837 3097
bookshop@fiveleaves.co.uk

www.fiveleavesbookshop.co.uk

The Book Hive is a wonder both for books and the soul, so everyone should go there, often – Eimear McBride

One of the best bookshops I've ever been in – Ian McMillan

53 London Street, Norwich NR2 1HL
www.thebookhive.co.uk   01603 219268

THE EUROPEAN BOOKSHOP

The languages and literatures of Europe in the heart of London!

10% DISCOUNT when you bring this advert to the bookshop

5 WARWICK STREET • LONDON • W1B 5LU
Tel: 020 7734 5259 Email: mrg@esb.co.uk
www.europeanbookshop.com
Mon-Fri 9:30am - 6:30pm
Sat 10:am - 6:30pm • Sun 12:00pm - 5:00pm

bookartbookshop
artists books and small press publications

home to the aesthetically and bibliographically curious

Wednesday to Friday: 1-7pm
Saturday: 12-6pm

17 Pitfield St, London N1 6HB

020 7608 1333
www.bookartbookshop.com

Editorial

There is much that I find strange in these pages. The texts reach us from far-away lands of ideas; they are stories, poems, extracts from longer works and entire linked series of prose poems filtered by the sensibilities of strangers, passing sometimes through several filters and via several strangers before washing up, legible if not always entirely sensible, on this shore. This is writing from provinces not capitals, from unfashionable suburbs and satellite neighbourhoods. Some of it dallies seriously with lower-class genres and joyfully plays snakes and ladders with the classics. The rare and the beautiful are here.

Do I mention the translators? I have to mention the translators, for this job they do. Without Lorna Scott Fox I couldn't have known anything of the wildness beating through the mind of Mexican iconoclast Julián Herbert nor, without Sawad Hussain, the magic worlds of Salim Barakat, just for example. I hazard that you, therefore, are not likely to have had the pleasure either. I can read French and Portuguese, but it was their translators Alison Entrekin and Jacob Siefring who introduced me to Adriana Lisboa's poetry and Pierre Senges's city creation mythology, and likewise for all the other texts. Please note, though, that the translators are here as writers, the translations as great writing, and Luke Carman's story from west Sydney I consider no less translated than anything else in the magazine – or perhaps no less in need of a good translation. Whose work isn't?

In most cases, I have asked the translator to provide a personal fanfare, an appreciation of the writer and the work they are championing through recreation. In most cases, then, there is no need for further introduction from me. Only Salim Barakat's work struck me as so unexpected that I decided these chapters from his centaur novel merited commentary from not one but two expert handlers.

And this has been my feeling in commissioning these works and bringing them all together: the thrill and tease of the chase, the scent of a new colour native to another world, just around the next thicket (such thickets of rights, of linguistic or bureaucratic reach, of communication in general). When some works seemed about to give me the slip – somehow Ukrainian Taras Prokhasko's para-utopian vision charmed a reading group but did not end up in hard covers a few years ago – I became all the more determined to track them down, to pin down at least a corner, a mouthful in English, and share the sensations of them with other readers. So this issue of *Sonofabook* has become a compendium of my recent obsessions, of my quarry of the last year or so and, in some cases, of the years to come too. I hope you enjoy the reading and may be encouraged to join me on this never-ending velvet hunt.

Many thanks to CB editions for the unique opportunity of *Sonofabook*; also to And Other Stories, to the Fundación Pan Klub, to the publishers and other rightsholders, and to all my patient writers and their impatient readers.

Sophie Lewis

subscribe
www.cbeditions.com

ADRIANA LISBOA

Two Poems

from Parte da paisagem *(Illuminuras, 2014);*
translated from the Portuguese by Alison Entreken

Animais Delicados

Claro que não têm a menor importância
as tardes nubladas. O comentário serve para
tirar da palavra a trava
de proteção. Tanto que depois
falamos de Hermann Hesse,
universos paralelos, Edward Bernays.
Falamos dos caras que querem saber se
suas garotas tiveram orgasmos múltiplos
e quantos exatamente
pois essa é a medida de sua (deles) adequação.
Falamos do quadro que você pintou
inspirado no filme. Mencionamos
esta nossa fé torta, exonerado o dogma.
Numa revelação ao revés,
fica acertado que seremos tenazes antes
da extinção, como o leopardo-de-zanzibar
e o lobo-da-tasmânia. Aliás:
como se enganam os passantes
acreditando, pelo tom da nossa voz,
que somos animais delicados.

Delicate Animals

Of course the cloudy afternoons aren't
even remotely important: the comment
merely takes the safety lock
off words. We then
talk about Hermann Hesse,
parallel universes, Edward Bernays.
We talk about the guys who want to know if
their girls have had multiple orgasms
and how many exactly
since that is the measure of their (the guys') adequacy.
We talk about the painting you did
inspired by the film. We mention
this crooked faith of ours, freed of dogma.
In a back-to-front revelation,
we agree to be tenacious before
extinction, like the Zanzibar leopard
and the Tasmanian Devil. In fact:
how mistaken are passers-by,
believing, from our tone of voice,
that we are delicate animals.

Testando A Voz

Eu estava apenas testando a voz
– aquecendo os músculos, digamos,
ou talvez passando o tempo para
não ter de confrontá-lo. Não é curioso
esse paradoxo? O tempo nos deu
nacionalidades distintas,
que é mais ou menos como sinto
esse buraco entre gerações,
mas enviamos gritos,
às vezes nos entricheiramos ali, às vezes
mandamos pombos-correio um para o outro
com cartas de alforria.
Em geral somos dóceis, embora o seu ar
distraído não me engane – a sua estratégia
de desligar os ouvidos. Em geral
somos os bichos domesticados que você e
os da sua geração tanto temiam. Cheguei
a pensar em agarrar suas roupas
e fazer coincidir nossos tempos.
Em vez disso, apenas abaixei os olhos
e disse boa noite e você nunca
ficou sabendo a que país eu pertencia
por trás das minhas mãos ao volante.

Testing My Voice

I was just testing my voice
– warming up, so to speak,
or perhaps killing time so I wouldn't
have to confront you. Isn't it curious,
this paradox? Time has given us
different nationalities,
which is pretty much how I feel
this gap between generations,
but we sling cries, sometimes
we take to the trenches, or
send messenger pigeons to one
another with proclamations of emancipation.
Most of the time we're docile, though your absent-
mindedness doesn't fool me – your strategy
of switching off your ears. Most of the time
we're the tame creatures that you and
those of your generation feared so much. I thought:
what if I grabbed you by the sleeve
and made our times coincide?
Instead, I just lowered my eyes
and said good night and you never
knew what country I belonged to
behind my hands on the steering wheel.

EMMANUELLE PAGANO

Two Stories

'Maman au Parc' and 'Juste un papa' from Un Renard à mains nues, © P.O.L. Editeur, 2012; translated from the French by Jennifer Higgins

Mum at the Park

On Sundays, I always wanted to go to the park in town with Mum. She preferred going to the river, not to the most popular parts but to places that only a few people knew about, peaceful places. I didn't want peace, though. I wanted to kick a ball around with my friends. A peaceful place, for my mother, meant somewhere she could read. She never used to play with me, and barely even talked to me, just as she barely talked to anyone, except when necessary, except, just sometimes, to her children. I was the youngest of the three, the little boy who still needed to play.

Mum didn't like the park because of the people. Not simply because they were there, stopping her being alone, but because the people in this park were worse than other people. They were dirty and raucous, aimless and hard to shake off. All the poor people, so poor they didn't even have a driving licence, let alone a car, drifted to this park on Sundays, gravitating towards a big old lime tree surrounded by graffiti-scrawled benches. There were lots of spelling mistakes on the wooden benches, but not on the seemingly indestructible tree bark, and, rushing around the benches, jumping over them and squirming underneath them, there were always plenty of children. I liked that, and Mum wanted me to be happy, so we went there, abandoning the calm of the water and the riverbank, leaving behind the regular, comforting sounds of the current, the rustle of pages and the echoes of my solitary ball. Mum always said yes in the end. She would sit down underneath the lime tree holding a book she knew she wouldn't be able to read, a little orphan in her hands, but feeling the pleasure of seeing me smiling and playing with the other children.

On that particular Sunday there were lots of children with their dubious-looking parents, but also quite a few younger people without children, sprawled comatose on the benches, finishing off their night out in the middle of the afternoon in the shade of the lime tree, guarding their dogs and their beers with their feet. I could see the fearful, fed-up look on Mum's face as she sat down as far away from them as possible. One of them, awake, bored and already tired of life, started trying to chat her up. She replied politely that she wanted to read, and she did actually start to read, once she had encouraged me to get the balls out of the bag (a basketball and a football) and to go and introduce myself to the other children, who were also laden with balls and on the look-out, like me, like everyone, for new friends. But I wanted to talk to Jérémie. He had just introduced himself, holding out his suntanned hand, so I knew he was called Jérémie. He looked about the same age as my older brother, and Mum pointed this out. I've got a son your age, you know. He looked nice and he looked canny. He'd already worked out that if he wanted to seduce my mum, he had to win me over. He started to explain dribbles and passes to me, all sorts of things about football and basketball, and even lots of things that had nothing to do with football or basketball, things about sport that were the same in life: altruism, respect, team spirit, playing straight, sticking to the rules, getting along with others. And at the same time he told me about his own life, a life that was already slipping by, the abandoned sports studies diploma, the job he claimed to have as a sports coach, his problems. I could tell he was talking to Mum, really, but in just a few minutes he'd become my best friend in the whole park.

Mum tried to focus on her book, checking on me once in a while as subtly as possible so that Jérémie couldn't catch her eye. Whenever he did manage to, he would begin reeling off heavy-handed compliments about the blue of her eyes, that blue she had passed on to me, undiluted, a blue bluer than the river on a sunny day, the blue of a cloudless winter sky, astonishingly bright in her ageing face, worn by time and sadness. I was a bit jealous but only a bit, because I knew I was her favourite. I knew he didn't have a chance, and I made the most of his loneliness to play with him because she never wanted to play with me.

She had used up all her patience with my brother and sister and I don't think she could stand any more ball games. She could only stand books and walks. She loved being with me, and going for walks with me. She loved me. She just didn't love the town, or the people in town, or the dirt in the streets and the park. Mum came from the countryside and always talked about how she longed for the moment when she could go back there, which irritated my older sister and me because we loved being here, near the shops and the rough part of town, the basketball hoops and the goalposts. Our brother lived in an even bigger town which seemed a dream land to us, or a fantasy land, as Mum said.

    When she was young, she didn't play the same sorts of games as we did. She gazed at the trees, did jigsaw puzzles without getting bored, spent lots of time drawing, and already read a lot. She lived alone with her dad in such an isolated place that it took hours to go and visit her mum. It was so far from the city crowds that you could tell when one of your neighbours was passing by listening for the sound of them walking in the snow, counting the number of steps by the dry, tearing sounds, shocking in the silence. Mum used to say that silence doesn't exist, that there are always tiny sounds in the background, muted and barely perceptible. And she was an expert in barely perceptible things. Her whole childhood was made up of them. Mum had red, prematurely aged hands, as if she'd been a cleaner, a labourer or a farmer, but she hadn't done any of those things. She just took so little care of herself, her hands, her face, anything to do with her appearance, so little care that it was almost a bit strange, as though she wanted people to think she was someone else. I gazed at her hands holding the book and missed a pass from Jérémie. His little dog started barking and jumping around like a mad thing.

My distraction was driving the puppy mad with excitement, as though each kick I missed pressed a button on a remote control linked to his tiny body, and he kept rushing, a noisy bundle of energy, after the lost ball. I followed this joyful little dynamo, forgetting Mum for a minute or two, but when Jérémie began to tell me about how his dog had picked up the scent of a fox the day before, as it was nosing through the bins, I turned to her straight away with a knowing smile. When she was a little girl, Mum had killed a fox with her bare hands to put an end to its suffering. She had often told us about this memory and, more often still, we had asked her to tell the story again and again. It seemed astounding to me that a fox could stray into town: a sign that it was time to go back to Mum. She looked at me and returned my smile, but held a finger on her lips to say that we should keep that story in the family. I felt the same. She got a snack out of her bag for me. She never forgot the snacks or the water or the books. Or even the balls.

I ran over to sit next to her, and Jérémie said goodbye, leaving us a carton of apple juice and making one final attempt to get Mum's number. He woke his friends and whistled to the dogs. They all left without closing the gate and as they went out another dog came in, an old, white dog with wobbly hind legs. He didn't have any of the bounce or playful barks of a young dog, but that didn't stop him chasing after the ball with me once I had finished my sandwich and Mum had picked up her book again.

Just a Dad

When I was a little girl I had to see a therapist because I'd killed a fox with my bare hands. I was happy to go along with it, but I never really saw the therapist because he always had his back to me, and in any case it wasn't all that terrible, the thing with the fox, or at least, it was terrible, but I thought I was doing the right thing. It was caught in a trap and couldn't get away. It was dying, and I just pressed its neck hard, crying the whole time, to make it die more quickly. To loosen the snare of sobs that was choking me.

My parents had just separated, and then there was the business with the fox, and my age, nine, so there was no getting round it: off to the shrink for me.

Mum was annoyingly keen on having everything arranged just right. She was frighteningly well-organised, and the therapist was the same, so between them they worked out a way of getting the most out of our journeys back and forth. Dad had stayed up at the top of the mountain, where we all used to live together when everything was still all right, and Mum had moved down to the bottom, to a village in the valley where the weather was milder. I lived with Dad during the week, and every weekend it felt as though I was swapping seasons. On Fridays after school, Dad took me to Mum's house, and Mum drove me back up on Sunday evenings. I was reunited with the winter, and with my dead tree, the one that had fallen down shortly before the divorce and that I used to play in until darkness began to fall, and sometimes long after. I'd made a den in its huge trunk. It had been famous, that tree, briefly. Someone had even written a book about it. When the therapist called to fix a time for my appointments, he mentioned that he drove up to see another child in a village halfway along the mountain road on Fridays, so Mum seized on that straight away – couldn't they meet there, my dad and my therapist, halfway, and make use of the journey time? He would pick me up in that village, and the session would take place in the car, as we drove down to Mum's house.

The therapist was a transition between Dad and Mum, and I really didn't like the way he drove, not one bit. He used to pick me up as arranged, at the mid-point, and I'd be worrying about all the twists and turns in the road before we even set off.

We would talk without looking at one another. There I was, imprisoned in the car seat, held fast by the seatbelt, telling his back all about my misfortunes. As we wound along the mountain road a slight nausea permeated my words. The therapist wasn't a very good driver and he didn't negotiate the bends as well as my parents did. The downward plunges frightened me. And anyway, being in a car with a man who was almost a stranger driving in front of me brought back bad memories of a time when I'd been horribly afraid, so horribly afraid that I'd forgotten all about the fear of being told off afterwards.

The fox was grey. That winter had been extremely cold and the fox had a very thick coat with long, almost white, hairs on the outside and a thick, much darker, downy layer underneath, like a sort of warm shadow. It had stopped struggling when I found it, and had wrapped itself up in its thick, winter tail as though to sleep, but it wasn't sleeping, it was dying. It was giving off a strong smell of urine and violets, like all foxes do, but this smell went far beyond the usual flowery whiff. It was the smell of panic. The smell was what led me to it. Apart from that, it was just a grey hollow in the snow. When I lifted it up I saw that underneath, its body was black with blood where the snare had sunk deep into the flesh. It tried to bite me, but so slowly that I could tell it was already far gone. Gone beyond fear, just waiting. But this just waiting was horrible. I held it to me and felt the faint beating of its heart. I couldn't manage to loosen the snare, which just cut straight through my gloves, and anyway I didn't want to free it; it was too late. I tried to use the metal wire to finish it off but it was impossible. I took off my shredded gloves and strangled it with my bare, frozen hands.

Before I did it, I stared at my gloves for a long time. They weren't gloves any more, just padded tatters. I wasn't afraid of what Dad would say, not at all, but I couldn't tear my eyes away from this bunch of rags, all torn to shreds like the fox's coat. And my hands, too, I looked at my hands, bizarrely white and intact. The fingers of my gloves were damaged but I was unscathed. I just had cold hands; my hands, fingers, palms, nails, wrists, all were smooth, firm, pale and naked. I looked at my torn gloves and my ungloved hands. My bare hands.

I put them on its neck as though to warm them, or to warm it. I pressed as hard as my youth would allow.

Seeing the therapist always reminded me of the moment I'd been most frightened in my whole life. That moment wasn't the one with the fox. It wasn't even in winter. It was a simple, summer fright, on a very hot day. The summer I turned six, a man picked me up in his car. He was looking for the police station and I knew where it was because my grandad was a policeman. I was in the village with Granny and had let go of her anxious hand. The man came up to me. I don't know what got into me, but I suddenly forgot all the well-worn phrases that Granny, Mum and Dad used to recite about not talking to strangers. I'd never really known what a stranger was. I didn't know what one would look like, how old he'd be, what sort of clothes he'd wear. So I wasn't suspicious of this one because I didn't know he was one. I got into his car with him so I could show him the way more easily, and I wasn't scared until he suddenly jammed the brakes on in front of the police station and asked me to get out, just in case people thought . . . I looked at him and realised what could have happened. I started to panic as I undid my seatbelt, and I ran all the way to my grandparents' flat.

The therapist was looking for a link between the fox and the stranger. I thought he was stupid. He was the one who was like the stranger: I didn't know him but there I was, sitting just behind him. Every Friday I sat behind the stranger, every Friday I got out of the car at my Mum's house as the stranger sat at the wheel. He was a bad driver. It made my stomach churn. Ups and downs inside me. For a therapist, he wasn't very good at analysing things. He kept saying that he wasn't a stranger, that I did know him. And then in a different voice he would say that I still hadn't told him anything about the fox. I never replied. He would ask if the fox was a symbol of fear, and if I knew what a symbol was. I would just smile and then (and it was exactly like this, every Friday) he would start to talk about my parents, about their separation, and my rather wild, isolated life with my dad. The fox, the symbol and dad. In that order. But the fear of the fox wasn't my fear. It was the fox's. The fox was afraid, not me.

One day I'd really had enough, and I suddenly asked him, right in the middle of telling the story of the summer I spent with Granny and Grandad when I was six, whether he'd noticed the road man. We'd just driven right past him. I asked if he'd seen him waiting for his dead to return, there on the bend, leaning against the safety barrier. The therapist said he was harmless, that everybody knew him and that I shouldn't be scared of him. I should stop being so interested in strangers. He looked at me in the rearview mirror and asked a thousandth question about the fox. When I didn't reply, he started going on about Dad's big beard.

He had it all completely wrong. Dad's beard was clean and soft. Dad wasn't some crusty old hermit living in the mountains, he was just a dad, just the only one who hadn't made a big fuss about my cold hands thawed by the grey, still-warm throat, my cold hands full of the smell of death and the winter fox. He hadn't even told me off about my ruined gloves. He had hugged me and comforted me, telling me about his own memories of childhood and of foxes. Then we had gone to find the corpse, taking a pair of pliers to cut the snare, and we'd dug deep into the ground below the snow and buried it. He had even cut off a hank of grey fur, which I added to the little store of treasured memories that I kept in the trunk of my tree and that, later, would help me comfort my own children when they were upset. My Dad knew just what to do, just what to talk about and what not to talk about, all those things the therapist would never understand.

Nathalie Léger

SUITE FOR BARBARA LODEN

Translated from the French by Natasha Lehrer and Cécile Menon

'It takes both the novel and biography to new and interesting places.'– Eimear McBride, *Guardian* Books of the Year, 2015

'A moving, subtle novel about the need to create' – *Le Monde*

'Brilliant little book' – Valeria Luiselli

LesFugitives
www.lesfugitives.com

Book and Kitchen is an artisanal bookshop with a small cafe and events space - hosting literary evenings, supper clubs, music nights and more. Combining the literary and culinary in a fresh and modern setting

BOOK & KITCHEN
31 ALL SAINTS ROAD, NOTTING HILL
LONDON W11 1HE
020 3417 8266
www.bookandkitchen.com

PIERRE REVERDY

Au soleil du plafond / Sun on the Ceiling

1916 (published 1955); translated from the French by Dan Bellm

Moulin à café

Sur la nappe il y avait quelques grains de poudre ou de café. La guerre ou le repos sur les fronts qui se rident ensemble. L'odeur mêlée aux cris du soir, tout le monde ferme les yeux et le moulin broyait du noir comme nos têtes. Dans le cercle des voix, un nuage s'élève. Une vitre à la lèvre qui brouille nos pensées.

Figure

Contre le mur des places vides. On risque de glisser sur ce plan qui remue. L'ombre soutient le poids, les doigts percent le nombre. Il y a un temps pareil à l'autre, au bout du monde. On pense à quelqu'un d'autre et, sur le marbre, on laisse un simple nom, sans préface ni point. Le portrait de sa vie. Mémoire. Il est content – Tout ce qui reste encore à faire en attendant.

Coffee mill

A few grains of powder or coffee on the tablecloth. War or repose on faces frowning together. The smell mingled with evening's cries, everyone's eyes shut, the mill grinding up blackness, our heads, too, grinding it. In the circle of voices, a cloud lifts. A glass at the lips to fog our thoughts.

Figure

Against the wall, empty spaces. A person could slip on this shifting surface. Shadow bears weight, fingers make holes in number. One time the same as another, at the far end of the world. A person thinks of another and leaves a simple name on the marble without preface or end point. The portrait of his life. Memory. He is happy: everything still to be done while waiting.

La pipe

Sous le nuage épais la voix monte vers le plafond dans un rond de fumée – comme son auréole. La voix et la fumée qui sortent de la pipe ou des lèvres minces et brûlantes. L'air de la chanson dans la nuit. Les intervalles de silence – et le feu qui s'éteint au moment où le bruit remonte des cascades fraîches de la bouche.

Musicien

L'ombre, le musicien, l'immense rideau bleu qui partage l'espace. C'est son nom qui frappe le battant, c'est l'air qui glisse mieux. Assis sur le versant profond d'une colline, entre les murs en creux, j'entends courir les signes plus vite que mes yeux. Entre les murs, devant le ciel, la fenêtre au milieu, les pieds sur le tapis où s'éteignent les étincelles, ou les étoiles, ou quelques autres signes lumineux.

The pipe

Under the dense cloud the voice rises to the ceiling in a ring of smoke – its halo. The voice and the smoke coming out of the pipe or out of thin burning lips. An air of song in the night. Intervals of silence – and the fire going out just as sound reascends the mouth's cool streams.

Musician

The shadow, the musician, the immense blue curtain dividing space. It's his name knocking at the door, an air floating forth. Sitting in the cleft of a hill between walls, I hear signals racing faster than my eyes. Between the walls, in front of the sky, window in the middle, feet on the carpet where sparks go out, or stars, or other luminous signs.

Le livre

La feuille au papier blanc, neuf sur la palissade. On monte et l'on descend.

La montagne est un livre dont les héros vont sur le vent. Les pages tournent, les mots tombent souvent.

Un bruit de tonnerre roule sur les pavés. C'est là que survient l'accident. Le livre est fait. Les hommes montent, une tranche sous chaque bras.

Contre le mur, l'auteur inquiet qui regarde vivre le monde et ne suit pas.

Papier à musique et chanson

La portée musicale et l'instrument des mots.

Le titre bref entre le côté droit et l'angle. Sur le plan blanc, les lignes courent et c'est la place que l'on tient dans la maison qui joue. Mais, si le son déborde, dehors c'est une autre chanson. Une nouvelle note et les rayons du ciel qui règlent l'écusson. Le mur, de l'arbre au toit, de la porte au balcon. La voix un peu plus haute.

The book

The white paper leaf newly grown on the fence. One climbs up and climbs down.

    The mountain is a book whose heroes travel the wind. The pages turn. Words often fall.

    The sound of thunder rolls over the paving stones. That's where the accident happens. The book is done. Men climb up, one section of it under each arm.

    Leaning against the wall, the anxious author watches the world live and does not follow.

Music paper and song

The musical stave and the instrument of words.

    The brief title between the right side and the corner. Lines run across the white surface, and it's the place one keeps in the house that plays music. But if the sound spills over outdoors it's another song. A new note, sunbeams marking lines on the coat of arms. The wall, from the tree to the roof, from the door to the balcony. The voice a little higher.

Guitare

Tout est calme dans l'air – cependant encore gonflé de bruit. La chanson d'hier lançait toujours ses vagues dans non têtes – et les airs à venir. Une pointe de l'aile s'enfonce au creux de l'abat-jour et son reflet caresse un instrument muet qui penche sur la table – Sourdes notes du souvenir.

Homme assis

Le tapis vert couché sous l'âtre c'est un piège.
 L'homme au profil perdu s'écarte du mur blanc. Est-ce le ciel qui pèse aux bras du fauteuil ou une aile. L'espace devient noir. Les murs sortent des lignes et coupent l'horizon. Après la course au faîte des maisons. Après l'espoir de revenir au signe on tombe dans un trou qui creuse le plafond. Les mains sortent à l'air. Le visage s'affine et tout rentre dans l'ordre, le cadre, le repos aux reflets d'encre et d'or.

Guitar

The air is all quiet, but still swollen with sound. Yesterday's song was still hurling its waves into our heads, and songs to come. A tip of its wing sinks into the lampshade, its reflection caressing a silent instrument that leans at the table. – Muffled notes of remembrance.

Seated man

The green carpet laid out at the hearth is a trap.
    The man with no silhouette steps away from the blank wall. Is it the sky weighing down on the arms of the chair or a wing. The space grows dark. Walls leave their lines and cut off the horizon. After running over rooftops. After hoping to come back to the sign and falling through a hole in the ceiling. Hands go out into the open air. The face grows thin and everything returns to normal, a restful tableau with glints of ink and gold.

Violon

Le tiroir repoussé, la porte refermée, les mains s'attardaient seules dans l'espace – les yeux toujours ouverts, un écho tremblant encore à nos oreilles. Déjà le violon s'était tu quand les pieds, que l'on ne voyait pas, continuaient à battre la mesure sous la table. Frontières dépassées, notes perdues dans l'air, tous les fils dénoués au-delà des saisons reprennent leur tour et leur ton sur le fond sombre du silence.

Éventail

Au mur des rangs de têtes, les épaules voûtées, les yeux sur les rainures et les pieds battant la mesure sur le parquet. Les mêmes traces pour les mêmes compas. On attend le signal, les rides lasses et les rideaux trop bas.

Il y a quelqu'un qui tourne dans la pièce à côté et ce n'est pas un bal. Mais contre la tenture un visage fermé – et la main qui glisse sur la bouche – un éventail inquiet.

Violin

Once the drawer was closed and the door shut, hands lingered alone in space – eyes open all the while, an echo still trembling in our ears. The violin had gone quiet but the feet, out of sight, kept beating time under the table. Borders transcended, notes lost in the air, all the threads undone beyond seasons retaking their measure and their tone on the dark background of silence.

Fan

A wall lined with heads and stooped shoulders, eyes on gaps in the parquet floor, feet beating time. The same tracks, the same pair of compasses. Waiting with slackened faces for the cue to begin, curtains hung too low.

Someone is moving around in the next room and it is not a dance. But against the drapery a closed-up face – and a hand gliding over the mouth – a restlessly waved fan.

La lampe

Le vent noir qui tordait les rideaux ne pouvait soulever le papier ni éteindre la lampe.

Dans un courant de peur, il semblait que quelqu'un pût entrer. Entre la porte ouverte et le volet qui bat – personne! Et pourtant sur la table ébranlée une clarté remue dans cette chambre vide.

Damier

Sur l'ordre du regard au plit trop net de la moulure les carrés blancs et noirs où se posent les doigts, le bout des ongles. C'est un chemin tracé entre ce cadre étroit et moi qui perds la tête. Un buisson où se cache l'endroit où passent les murmures. Dans la salle d'été avec un feu éteint le plafond ramassé et deux grosses figures les yeux baissés.

The lamp

The dark wind that twisted the curtains couldn't lift up the paper or put out the lamp.
 In a gust of fear it seemed someone had managed to come in. Between the open door and the banging shutter – nobody! And yet over the rattling table a brightness stirs in this empty room.

Checkerboard

On the order of a glance at the molding too neatly arranged, black and white squares where fingers and fingertips rest. A path laid out between this narrow space and me losing my mind. A bush where the place of passing murmurs hides. In the summer room with the squat roof and the fire gone out, two fat characters with downcast eyes.

Soupière

Le monde de la faim, la fin du monde. La soupière est comme un globe terrestre sur la table. Et du globe fendu couvercle soulevé, l'odeur monte et une tête et des bras blancs dans un nuage.

Et la tête riait – la tête riait et flottait d'un bout à l'autre de la table.

Du parfum à la faim, par un chemin plus long, ramenant les ardeurs du fond d'un autre songe.

Enveloppe

Le temps remis la marche des refrains guide l'allure.

Pour la nuit, c'est le cercle des visages nus sous l'attraction des sortilèges de la lampe. Les profils dégagés du long talus de pierres où l'ombre s'épaissit sur la rivière molle. Sous l'arc, un oiseau passe, comme un souvenir en retard, les gestes dépassés et détachés du nombre au moment du départ. Je marque le nom propre au revers du destin, de l'enveloppe sombre à l'aile du hasard.

Tureen

The world of hunger, the end of the world. The tureen like a globe on the table. And from the cracked-open globe with its raised lid an odor rises, a head and white arms in a cloud.

    The head laughed – the head laughed and floated from one end of the table to the other.

    From aroma to hunger, by a longer path, drawing up ardors from the depths of another dream.

Envelope

The restarted time of refrains sets the pace.

    For the night, it's the circle of naked faces under the lamplight's spell. Loosened sections of the long stone embankment where darkness thickened over the sluggish river. A bird passes under the arch like a memory come late, the casual old gestures of number at the moment of departure. I write the proper noun on the other side of fate, on the back of the dark envelope on the wing of chance.

Compotier

Une main, vers les fruits dressés, s'avance et, timidement, comme une abeille, les survole. Le cercle où se glissent les doigts est tendu dessous comme un piège – puis reprennent leur vol, laissant au fond du plat une cicatrice vermeille. Une goutte de sang, de miel au bout des ongles.

Entre la lumière et les dents, la trame du désir tisse la coupe aux lèvres.

Jet d'eau

La silhouette au bec retourné découpe un large pan sur la muraille. Tout le ciel dans le verre qui passe par devant. L'espace reste bleu. Sur le meuble, une plaie livide et des carrés poudreux. Le jet d'eau creuse l'air, la vapeur sort des lignes et le bruit de la mer se calme peu à peu.

Fruit bowl

A hand reaches toward the arrangement of fruit and, timid as a bee, hovers over it. The circle where the fingers glide is drawn tight as a trap – then they resume their flight, leaving at the bottom of the dish a bright red scar. A drop of blood, honey on the fingertips.

    Between light and teeth, the web of desire binds the bowl to the lips.

Fountain

The silhouette with the upside-down mouth carves a wide swath on the wall. The whole sky inside the glass that passes in front of it. The space remains blue. A bluish scar on the furniture, and patches of dust. The jet of water bores a hole in the air, vapor strays outside the lines, the sound of the sea subsides slowly.

Pot de fleurs

Le vague des rideaux derrière le balcon où jamais ne s'accoude personne.

Silhouettes de jour, masse épaisse de nuit, des drames sans éclat qu'encadre la fenêtre. Puis, un coup de soleil, une fusée de rires et dans la rue déserte, entre les deux trottoirs, une pluie de couleurs, une avalanche de pétales, gouttes qui s'évaporent et parfument le vent.

Masque

Au fond du verre, l'œil fixe, le ruban, la goutte d'or et un regard qui tremble. Tout le monde est parti. Ce triste carnaval entre l'hiver et l'âtre, le soleil réchauffant. La pluie tombe plus doucement, la mer se décolore et le visage dur redevient transparent. Sous les traits découverts, la tête est à la mode. Et même dans la glace contre le paravent. Ma mémoire en désordre.

Flowerpot

The rippling of curtains behind the balcony no one leans on.

    Silhouettes by day, mass of darkness by night, lifeless dramas framed by the window. Then a burning sun, a burst of laughter, and in the deserted street between two sidewalks, a shower of color, a hail of petals, droplets that turn to mist and scent the air.

Mask

In the bottom of the glass, the fixed gaze, the ribbon, the drop of gold, and a trembling glance. Everyone has gone away. Sad carnival between winter and hearth, the warming sun. The rain falls more softly, the sea is drained of color, and the harsh face becomes transparent again. Beneath its naked features, the head is fashionable. Even in the mirror against the folding partition. My disordered memory.

Bouteille

La bouteille au centre de feu, à bout de bras ou sur la table. Dans la forme des mains, dans la source des poches – il y a de l'or et de l'argent – il y a de l'esprit dans la manche. Quand la couleur coule à pleins bords – quand l'air s'embrouille dans les branches. Le cœur va plus loin que les yeux, la flamme renaît de la cendre. Entre le fil qui coule et le trait lumineux les mots n'ont plus de sens.
    On n'a plus besoin des mots pour se comprendre.

Pendule

Dans l'air chaud du plafond la rampe des rêves s'allume.
    Les murs blancs se sont arrondis. La poitrine oppressée souffle des mots confus. Dans la glace, tourne le vent du sud chargé de feuilles et de plumes. La fenêtre est bouchée. Le cœur est à peu près éteint parmi les cendres déjà froides de la lune – les mains sont sans abri – tous les arbres couchés. Dans le vent du désert les aiguilles s'inclinent et mon heure est passée.

Bottle

The bottle in the middle of the fire, at arm's length or on the table. In the shape of hands, in the wellspring of pockets – there is silver and gold – there's a spirit up the sleeve. When color runs freely, when air is tangled in branches. The heart goes farther than the eyes, flame is reborn from ash. Between the flowing thread and the stroke of light, words stop making sense.

No more need of words to make ourselves understood.

Clock

In the warm air on the ceiling the footlights of dreams switch on.

The blank walls swell out. The troubled breast gasps out muddled words. The south wind spins inside the mirror, packed with feathers and leaves. The window is blocked. The heart is almost snuffed out amongst the moon's cold ashes – hands without a place to rest – all the trees asleep for the night. In the desert wind the hands point straight down and my time is up.

| PASSIONATE ABOUT PAMPHLETS

AWOL, by John Fuller and Andrew Wynn Owen

Two poets write each other letter-poems on the subject of travel.

True Tales of the Countryside, by Deborah Alma

Eyeballs pop, fresh piss steams and women come – loudly – in this rich, pungent debut from Deborah Alma, aka the Emergency Poet.

Visit our website for information about our books, events & calls for submissions
WWW.THEEMMAPRESS.COM

Have you 'got a book in you'?

If so, good news – independent publisher Valley Press is searching for new writing throughout 2016, with our biggest-ever 'call for submissions'. If you've written (or are writing) a book/pamphlet of poetry, fiction or non-fiction, we want to hear from you. For details, see **valleypressuk.com/submissions**

JULIÁN HERBERT

Two Stories, One Poem

from Cocaína: Manual del usuario (Cocaine: A User's Manual, *Almuzara, 2006);
translated from the Spanish by Lorna Scott Fox*

Sitting in Baker Street

Call me Sherlock Holmes. I am sitting in Baker Street, alternating from week to week between cocaine and ambition. My fingers occupy their astonishing strength in grinding rocks and preparing needles. The acute precision of my pupils ensures that nothing is spilt, that the dose is exact despite the tremors that afflict me and the droning in my ears. The peculiar dimensions of my skull are nothings: idle, glistening nothings curved like a slide, a toboggan run on which the brutalities of logic falter and collapse. I am sitting in Baker Street, watching the dirty carriage wheels roll through the snow.

Call me Adam. I am sitting in Baker Street, deep in my armchair of leather and wood. I am naked. My cock is the sweetest in all Creation. My cock is asleep and I can't seem to wake it up. I tried watching porn films, nothing. I tried shaking it beneath a spout of icy water, nothing. I tried thinking about you, still nothing: nothings as idle and glistening as a gramme on a piece of paper. I have a sweet and useless cock, a lightning bolt of flesh that's fading out. If we could just make love tonight. In the meantime, anyway, pass me that little mirror on top of the sink.

Call me Georg Trakl. I am sitting in Baker Street. My body is a pharmacy. Anis and devil's sugar. My dried-out bones lie scattered on Grete's lap. The glistening nothing of desire. Ambiguity and muck. Salzburg through the window, its streets, its dank breath leaping like a batrachian to hide down every throat. The jars on the shelves:

laudanum, placebos and syrups. The wallpaper is smudged all over with my finger-marks, the marks of staggering and falling night after late night, peering at my nails, masturbating with difficulty over an old mantilla my sister left behind her that October afternoon. One of these days I'm off to Borneo. Here comes another salvo.

Call me Antonio Escohotado. I am sitting in Baker Street, it's two in the morning and I'm still deep in documents: a passage where the Inca Garcilaso describes ritual offerings of coca; a prospectus in which Dr Freud recommends the new product from Merck; a screed against the clinical use of morphine, laudanum and heroin; a chemical report on the *French Wine of Coca, Ideal Tonic* which J. S. Pemberton sold years later to Asa Candler under a fizzing name: *Coca-Cola*. Outside in the square – I can half spy on them through the net curtain – two boys are taking it up the arse in exchange for a hit. I'm sitting in Baker Street watching the dirty wheels of history roll through the snow.

Call me I. I'm sitting in Baker Street. I spend my money on the blow that keeps my lungs going in and out. All oxygen is a nasal circuit: the bin full of Kleenex, Kleenex full of blood, Kleenex full of me. I turn on the computer. I play solitaire until my left hand goes numb. Then I try to write. Then I look at the clock: twenty minutes have passed. I go into the bathroom, sit astride the toilet, tap a little powder onto the mirror and then a little more. I sniff at it, break it up with my Serfín bank card and make two long lines, nice and thick. I inhale. Every day like that. I've got through almost a third of an ounce, haven't slept for don't know how many hours, I don't know how to stop. They're going to sack me. Call me what you like: cokehead, junkie, sick, whatswrongwithyouson, giveitarestmate, deadoralivewhocares, call me scum and call me god, call me by my name and the name of my headaches, the name of my reading until it gets light and me here desperate. I'm the one scrabbling for crumbs under the desk, under the sink, on the mirror, on my shirt, and it's getting light again and not a bean, and the cold smirk of the neighbour through the blinds, like you think they haven't noticed.

I'm sitting in Baker Street watching the dirty wheels of my life roll through the snow.

Call me Ishmael: I'm sitting in Baker Street, by the fire, trying to hunt an enormous white animal with my words. It measures almost a league in length, its tail is pure foam, its eyes possess the heaviness and glitter of the fiercest salt. It's an animal prone to fear and fury, it kills blindly, and when it doesn't kill you it splits your life apart. But it's also a lucid and beautiful beast, with breath like music, and at the moment when its tail lashes you and flings your body into the air you're not thinking about the pain or the drip of blood: you're only thinking about the speed – which is like not thinking, or not feeling yourself think, or sitting in the middle of the purest snow watching the dirty wheels roll by.

Call me Ishmael. I am here to tell you a story.

Rubbish Batting

It doesn't matter if you're a priest or a drunk or a fag or a cop. It doesn't matter if you live in Colonia del Valle or Hong Kong or Las Gradas or the moon. It doesn't matter if your hobby is writing speeches, killing Arabs, catching oysters in Guaymas, cleaning toilets in Durango or fucking stunted girls in hotels off Calzada de Tlalpan. I totally agree with you about one thing: what there's most of in the air is oxygen and bastards. And I'm not just saying that to please you, no, let alone to make you think that you and I are better, nothing like that: I mean it completely seriously. And luminous people do appear from time to time, as you well know.

There's this tenement where I drop by to score sometimes. Dopey's room is at the back. It's pretty squalid, just a bed, some girlie posters, a scale, bags of powder and rocks, and under the mattress, I reckon, more dosh than you or I could earn by working for months. To reach that room you have to go along a roofless passage. There you get kids playing footie, women hanging out the washing and sixteen-year-old chicks slouched against the doors to either side, checking out the Avon catalogue. You know, all that crap they go for with the hand-held cameras and grainy resolution in our so-called New Mexican Cinema.

At the end of the passage, outside the door where Dopey does business, sits Don Chago. He's always in his council street-sweeper uniform, though you can tell by the way he moves that he's retired. He's holding a transistor radio to his ear with the schizophrenic voice of a sports announcer squeaking out.

'Hey Don Chago, how's it going?'

He pats his forehead with a red paisley square and answers:

'Nothing, same as ever, just bloody rubbish batting.'

I never dare ask if he means anyone in particular. Instead: I snort a line, and then another, now I can feel in my skin how the fielders stumble after the base hits, Houston Jiménez cracks a plastic cup between his fingers, Don Chago wipes his face with a damp square and looks sullenly at his radio and the girls do their strict sums and still can't make it to the nail varnish or eyeshadow duo.

Trashed and thrashed every night. Losers together.

Zapatistas in the Bathroom

oh baby I can't tell you what an awful night
I was happy thinking about you
writing a poem about the spring
a friend came round and asked me to put up
3 or 4 Zapatistas who were in town
oh my love I said yes happily
still thinking about you
still writing my poem

I didn't know no I didn't know
that I'd be tangling with Mexico's rough

they gave a talk and I dozed off fine
but then when they came back here it was a scam
it wasn't 3
it was 10
and not one of them a Zapatista
their trades did strike me as very strange
    4 punks
    1 teeshirt vendor
    2 orthodox Marxists infiltrated into Telmex
    2 skanky Europeans but from nice families
and the tenth I guess had probably been a boxer
because once sloshed he lost all respect

but the saddest thing baby
ah honey
is that they all lived here in Monterrey
they'd only gone to Chiapas to
see a waterfall

as soon as they got settled they wanted food
they didn't care that I was thinking about you
and hadn't finished my poem
they looked at me contemptuously they called me
an individualist
then they put on a Def cassette and
after that the Ramones
they sang like they were throwing up

seeing they weren't going to relent I cooked
1 kilo of eggs 6 tomatoes 20 chillies 80 tortillas 2 bags of beans
they were chivvying me along

their eyes flashed
several litres of Tonayan dribbled from their mouths
the house stank like a mezcal sweat lodge

I was awake all night

drinking Coca-Cola

unable to take a piss because there were always
   (therewerealwaystherewerealways)

Zapatistas in the bathroom
Zapatistas in the bathroom

after some arguing
and throwing punches
and being rude about the government
and criticising Marcos
and praising the proletarian dictatorship of the street
after nodding off and vomiting burping expectorating and more
swinging at each other
drawing blood
from one another's muzzles
after assuring me that Zapata was
a queer
they went away at last with the hangover
you only get at 10 a.m.
they went away and the only forfeit
the only souvenir they left me
was a Violent Femmes cassette

so when they disappeared
like it had all been magic
or all just an old dream

spring crept over the hangover rankness
lily stems budded on your photos
flowers in your filthied hair
I felt madly like reciting poetry aloud
and that's when the best was still to come
oh honey
you came in on the heels of spring
with the private property of your little breasts
with the imperialistic checks of your green blouse
hey dear – you were ready
to play deal or no deal – and while you were undressing
I mentally forgave the exploiters who ate my food
vomited over my furniture and in exchange
only gave me
this lousy cassette
I suddenly knew I'd never be a rebel
I don't know who I am
so fickle
I'd settle for a drink
a glass bead and a cassette
I'd settle for a line
a blouse on the floor and a cassette

which is why I'm saying:
pass the little mirror so I can see myself up close
because I can't make out any more what's right
or what's wrong

Anthony Barnett at Allardyce Book

New for 2016 - 128 pp - 978-0-907954-53-8 - £15 incl. mailing
Sonofabook-reader offer: buy this book and receive Snow lit rev 4 free

Antonyms Anew: Barbs & Loves

Commentaries, many of which first appeared in *The Use of English* and *Tears in the Fence*, on mostly loved writers Andrea Zanzotto, Robert Musil, Joseph Roth, Osip Mandelstam, José Saramago, Edvard Munch, Louis-René des Forêts, Aimé Cesaire, D S Marriott, Bohumil Hrabal, Leopardi, Gunnar Ekelöf, Clarice Lispector, Cees Nooteboom, Valeria Luiselli, Witold Gombrowicz, Kajii Motojirō, Takashi Hiraide, Douglas Oliver, Natsume Sōseki, Victor Segalen, Samuel Beckett, Qian Zhongshu, Eileen Chang, Isak Dinesen, César Vallejo, Umberto Saba, J H Prynne, George Oppen, New York Art Quartet and Amiri Baraka, Knut Hamsun, Kawabata Yasunari, Fernando Pessoa, Czesław Miłosz, Julia Hartwig, Robert Walser, Roger Giroux, Ai Weiwei. One unusual piece, set in Doves Type revival, discusses typography; while another scrutinizes the unexpected surfacing in 2015 of a cache of letters written by Henry Crowder to Nancy Cunard.
As for the barbs they mostly catch the ways of certain publishers and certain translators

Poems &

poetry & prose 1968–2012, 978-0-907954-46-0, 658 pp, £48, or £36 with Translations

meticulous . . . striking . . . the weight of enigma presses down hard on
his poems, each in its way like an epitaph to a longer, unknown work
- Jeremy Harding in *TLS* on the earlier collected *The Resting Bell*

Translations

Akutagawa, Albiach, Delahaye, Des Forêts, Giroux, Lagerkvist, Vesaas, Zanzotto
& others, 978-0-907954-47-7, 342 pp, £36, or £25 with Poems &, both in assoc. *Tears in the Fence*

Anthony Barnett admits that he too "has to do what is difficult".
This sympathy helps him to avoid what des Forêts calls the trap
of seeing only the beauty of the world, and catch instead the
"ferocious harmonies" of "lifelong inconsolability"
- Andrew McCulloch in *TLS* on des Forêts *Poems of Samuel Wood*

Snow *lit rev 4 - spring 2016 - 192 pp - £15 or free with Antonyms Anew*
prose, poetry, music, art, film, photography, edited by Anthony Barnett and Ian Brinton
no. 1, spring 2013, *includes etching by* Gisèle Celan-Lestrange; *letter by* J H Prynne *on* Celan
no. 2, fall 2013–spring 2014, *includes* Anthony Barnett-George Oppen *letters*; Prynne *Shen Zhou*
no 3, spring 2015, *includes* Cees Nooteboom-Anthony Barnett *correspondence*; Zanzotto *essay*
no 4, spring 2016, *includes essay by* Takashi Hiraide *on the artist* On Kawara; Ponge; Segalen
visit www.abar.net/snow.pdf for downloadable content and subscription information

www.abar.net | Allardyce, Barnett, Publishers | ab@abar.net
07816 788442 | 14 Mount Street · Lewes · East Sussex BN7 1HL | 01273 479393

TARAS PROKHASKO
from *The Unsimple*

translated from the Ukrainian by Uilleam Blacker

Taras Prokhasko is one of post-Soviet Ukraine's most important writers, and surely one of the most unusual literary voices in Europe today. Ever since he published his first short stories in the mid-1990s, his prose has been unmistakable for its surprising subject matter and highly idiosyncratic style, both of which have won him a cult following among Ukrainian readers. Prokhasko's work is deeply philosophical, developing what could be described as its own particular phenomenology. What does it mean to inhabit the world, to exist in a specific place, to sense and feel the world around us? How do we use language to convey these experiences? These are the questions that lie at the heart of his work, and which give birth, on the one hand, to the startling explorations of sensuality, perception, and of human beings' interactions with the natural world that one finds in his prose, and on the other to his preoccupation with language, narrative and storytelling.

It is in relation to storytelling that the true significance of the mysterious Unsimple of his novel lies. These are strange figures, based in part on the phantoms and fantasies of Carpathian folklore, whose mission is to collect and weave the stories of individuals, families and nations, and who have the power to produce both beauty and tragedy. In the novel, the concept of storytelling is signified by the strange, small word bai *(pronounced like 'bye'). This is an odd little word in Ukrainian, appearing on its own only really in lullabies (by strange coincidence, it even appears in this English word!) and in the colloquial verb baiaty – to speak or tell stories. In the case of Prokhasko's novel* The Unsimple, *the principal story is a tragedy: to paraphrase Milan Kundera, the tragedy of Central Europe in the 20th century. This is a place of richness and diversity of culture and landscape, as evocatively captured by Prokhasko, but which suffered from being at the centre of the terrifying and destructive plots of war and totalitarianism. In many ways, Prokhasko's peculiar tale of a mountain resort in the centre of Europe is really a tale of unrealised narrative potential, of unfinished narratives, and of tales broken off in mid-sentence. It is perhaps this that gives Prokhasko's prose its unusual fragmented structure: the novel appears in many numbered fragments, like shards of objects uncovered in an archaeological dig, or the botanical specimens salvaged from a long-ago expedition, retrieved and numbered in a guessed order, and thus continually expressing potentiality of interpretation and narrative elaboration, but never providing a complete picture of reality.*

Prokhasko's work is fascinating and frustrating for the translator. His elliptical prose is a joy to read, but provides endless stumbling blocks in its inherent ambiguity, which is facilitated by the possibilities of free-ranging Ukrainian grammar but which precision-loving English often finds a challenge. Besides style, there is the question of cultural and geographical specifics. Prokhasko knows the Ukrainian Carpathians, their flora, topography, customs, languages and cultures, in minute detail, and some of the realia described in the novel may puzzle even the Ukrainian reader. A prime example of this is the exhaustive catalogue of strange names for the different designs used on pysanky, the traditional Ukrainian painted Easter eggs, which features in this excerpt. The accumulation of detail is such that the reader of the original feels truly submerged in the landscapes; I hope that the reader of this translation will have a similar experience.

The Unsimple was originally published in two parts by the journal Ukrainian Literature in Translation *in 2007 and 2011. The excerpt included here has been slightly altered and improved.*

— U.B.

The Unsimple

1 They said the Unsimple would come to the funeral. Why they hadn't appeared for so many years, when they had been truly needed, nobody knew. Obviously, it wasn't necessary for them. It meant that the death of the French Engineer interested them more than Ialivets during the war. Or perhaps the real war, outside Ialivets, was more interesting for them. Here, after all, nothing happened that the French engineer couldn't keep an eye on. If they really were still tied to Ialivets, then they would come in order to do two things: first, to collect something the French engineer had left behind, and second, to leave somebody in his place. Franzysk said that they were interested in certain people. Sebastian vividly recalled how Franz had shielded Anna from them, how he had spoken of the haunting of their family by the Unsimple. The fear that someone might take his (and his Anna's) daughter from him came – at least for a few seconds – every hour. Now it had become all-consuming and pushed Sebastian to his limits. They had to escape.

Anna slept, and Sebastian grated potatoes and fried some potato pancakes, so as to have something substantial to take on the journey.

He grated, fried, and thought about something completely different.

2 the unsimple are earthly gods. people who with the help of inborn or acquired knowledge are able to do good or harm to others. that point is important – inborn or acquired. they know something. at the same time this can also be learned. acquired. in this way it's possible to become unsimple by learning something.

and the inborn. they were interested in Anna's dreams. was this inborn or acquired. it came from the morphine – acquired. but it came only to Anna. the morphine uncovered something. which means –

inborn. Anna explained some things to me, I learned some things – acquired. Anna said that not everyone could master her teachings. there must be some kind of characteristics. characteristics are the principal stories. they're intonations. intonations make the voice. something innate and unchanging – it can at most be imitated. to imitate, one must know. imitation is knowledge, because knowledge is imitation. they were interested because Anna knew something they had not learned. which means their knowledge is not limitless. they have to acquire it. string it on to characteristics. unsimple are different. it's impossible for one person alone to acquire all knowledge. but each one for whatever reason chooses certain branches of knowledge. depending on characteristics. they are of all kinds – cowlike, horselike, catlike, doglike, chickenlike, gooselike, fishlike, froglike, mouselike. like all creatures that take nourishment from other creatures. there is also the snake charmer, the werewolf, the storm breaker, the cloud driver, the hill wanderer. there is also the seer and the seeress. but the most important is the *bai*-maker, the spellcaster. the most powerful is the spell – speaking, *bai*. *bai* – is not a word. *bai* – is many ordered words. a *bai* – is already a history. for different motivations there are different *bais*. *bais* are stories. a *bai* is a narrative, the narrating of a history, a story. motivations must also be stories. and in order to find a *bai* for them, they must be told. in this case narrative influences the choice of narrative and then the chosen narrative is narrated. the *bai* is narrated, the *bai* which influences, acts on the previous narrative-motivation and matches the direction in which it is going after the narrative-*bai* towards the narrative-effect. which means that there are only narratives. narrative is all actions, and all actions are narratives. among the unsimple the *bai*-maker is number one. his inborn knowledge-characteristics – how to narrate (hearing, articulation, voice, intonation, rhythm, pace) – are strung together with acquired ones – what to narrate. unsimple must know what to narrate. they need people's narrations – Anna's, the French engineer's, Beda's, deputy Stefanyk's, General Tarnavskyi's. what they know, they tell to someone else. but to whom. to Franzysk, Anna, Loci. afterwards

Franzysk makes films, Anna builds buildings, which then *bai* something to someone else. and these someones have something they have to re-*bai* to someone else. have to. unsimple do what they want. wanting also has to be known from somewhere. to know is to hear a narrative. wanting – narrative, *bai*. wanting is had. unsimple want to have. the best way to have – is to be able to narrate, to make narrations. whosoever narrates has everything. narration, therefore, is not only the greatest act, but also the greatest thing, the greatest number. the greatest characteristic and trait. unsimple have the most, do the most, signify the most, because they narrate. the mystery turned out very simple. knowing criminals A, crime B is dreamt up for them. unsimple rule the world. unsimple come when someone is born, or something is born, and think up its life. they narrate a plot. the narrative becomes the cause, life – the effect of the narrative. and the cause of a new narrative, which can be heard and retold. there is no life without narrative. because narrative is life. histories do not end, said Franzysk. stories hide and emerge. histories, like infections, cause fever, are carried, are passed on, hide, come out and cause fever. they merge, separate, mix together, grow together, break in different places, overturn, crumble, are reborn. to gather plots. to combine plots (analysis, synthesis, deduction, induction, mythologisation, de-mythologisation, analogy, hyperbole, addition, subtraction, multiplication, division, accent, timbre, articulation, transfer, cohesion, instillation, elimination, tonality, speed, rhythm, chronotope, personification, allegory, synonym, antonym, homonym, construction and deconstruction, comparative linguistics). to give away stories, according to place and time. such is the method of the unsimple. and this method is a result. for it is as it is said, ordered, related, refused, retold, forbidden, indicated, suggested. what is it for. in order to say.

bai is invisible medicine.

the essence of all form.

the form of essence itself.

that which can be taken into the next world. that which is necessary in the next world. for there is nothing but voices, eternity and delight.

your own eternity with your own voice your own *bai* about your own delight.
no work, no treasure, no strength, no body, no emotions, not far, not near, not much, not little, not sometime, not now, not sometime. your own eternity with your own voice your delight – your *bai*.

3 Sebastian gave all the potato pancakes to Anna for breakfast, because they had nowhere to go, because there was nowhere to escape to. The main thing is to fear nothing.

Sebastian went to the deceased, prayed (dear God, don't allow me to harm Thee!) for the narrative of the soul of the French engineer and waited until the Unsimple arrived. They asked him not to hinder them and to wait two days, although this family had for the first time sought them out, and not the other way round. Sebastian promised not to take up much time and stepped inside. He told the *bai*-maker that he wanted to be a *bai*-maker. And asked to work as a barman in the bar which belonged to the Unsimple.
At that time in Ialivets the bar 'Is As Is' had become the most fashionable post-war locale in a fashionable pre-war Central European resort. After the war the address changed a little, although things didn't pass off without some essential errors. Despite everything Ialivets was still situated in the Ukrainian Carpathians, and not simply in the Czechoslovak Republic. But Stanislaviv, Lviv and Ardzheliudzha were beyond the forbidden line through Chornohora. Now for Ialivets' gin people came mainly from Prague, Brno, Bratislava, Košice, Karlovy Vary and Uzhhorod. And also from Podebrady and Nusli, from Německý Jablonec, Liberec and Józefów. With the foreigners it was easier to communicate using Ukrainian than German.

The Unsimple without hesitation agreed, but had one condition. As it happened, Sebastian also had only one condition. Both conditions turned out to be the same – Anna should be in the bar, beside Sebastian.

The Temptations of Saint Anthony

1 Little Anna was given a miniature figure of St Anthony by the Unsimple. Anthony standing up straight, in a monk's habit; in one hand he holds lilies on long stems, in the other – a child. Despite his size, Anthony looked like a real statue when Anna laid her head on the floor and placed the figure a little distance away, or – still looking up from the floor – when she stood him on the very edge of a table. Especially striking was the expression of pure devotion in his facial features.

The Unsimple said Anthony had been cast from melted-down lead that had once been a bullet. The figure lived in a metal cylinder of the type soldiers use to keep tags with their names and the addresses of their families. Anna wore the cylinder around her neck on a long wire chain. From the constant rubbing of the copper her skin was always marked with green stains. Franzysk didn't consider this to be harmful. When the weather was especially fine, Anna would take Anthony for walks. She would take him out of his capsule and give him an airing somewhere in the grass. When she closed him back in she would place alongside him a little flower – a violet, a dog daisy, a plum or lime-tree blossom, so that Anthony didn't feel suffocated.

2 Anna herself smelled beautiful. Franz liked most of all when she fell asleep on his table. He would work on a while, though paying more attention to his curled-up, sleeping daughter than to his work, and then crawl up onto the table, put a book under his head, put his arms around Anna and lie for a long time breathing in the air that she breathed out. He stroked her head, and sometimes in the morning Anna would wake up with short, broad, light scratches on her skin where the calluses on Franzysk's fingers had lightly scraped her face.

3 Franzysk was convinced that there could not be a more worthwhile activity than watching his daughter. Every day he saw thousands of perfect images but for some reason never bothered to use his camera. As a consequence, he dedicated so much energy to memorising the images that he sometimes caught himself thinking he couldn't possibly go on like this. Very often by the evening he could remember nothing of what had happened during the day other than those imaginary photographs (although when Anna was a little older he could describe to her for hours how she had looked on any given day in her childhood).

4 Anna was six years old when she told her father that she could remember how she had once slept in a large box placed on a long trolley with eight wheels under a tree, from which hung a nest with an opening on its underside. The little hatch was open, and from inside the nest the blue eye of a bird had peered at her. And then from all sides flocks of little white owls had swooped down and landed in concentric circles around the tree on the ground, on the haystacks, on the dog-rose bushes, on the well and the hayrick. And also on the wires stretched from pole to pole.

5 Franzysk decided that such a vision must be the result of morphine use and called on the Unsimple. They had a talk with Anna, and eventually the seeress said that the little girl had dreamed it all. She warned Franz that the little one would begin to tell him more and more often of all kinds of wonders, would begin to ask whether or not this or that had once happened to her. That about certain things she would be unsure until death – what had happened and what was a dream – because for her there would be no real or unreal, just different types of reality. But dreams have nothing in common with seeing into the future. They tell us how things can be.

6 Franz decided that his daughter should know at least one thing in the world perfectly and without any doubts. They started

walking round Menchil Kvasivskyi to the Kevelov, which flowed into the Chorna Tysa, and Anna learned all the stones on its banks – how each one of them looked, and which lay by which.

In the meantime, the Unsimple crossed over the mountains and settled in Ialivets, and stayed there on and off right up until 1951, when a special Chekist unit, disguised as Ukrainian Insurgent Army soldiers, used flamethrowers to burn down the mental asylum where some of the Unsimple had been interned back in 1947. They had to get closer to Anna.

7 A few weeks before the beginning of the year 1900 Franz finished a very important animated film.
'To live is to untie and tie knots, with your hands and everything else,' he was once taught by an Unsimple snake charmer, who gave him a whole bundle of grass snake skins. Franz was to untangle the skins and weave his own pattern. Logic lives in the fingers, and its categories are defined purely by what the fingers are capable of. He turned the bundle over and over in his hands like a rosary for many days and nights. Eventually he untied all the knots, but when it came to making his own pattern his fingers found it terribly difficult not to follow the shapes already ingrained in the surface of the skins. Anna, on the other hand, tied such knots that the snake charmer decided to take Franz to the bridge where the Unsimple had made their home.

8 At one time they'd wanted to extend this viaduct from one side of the ridge to the other, across the place where Ialivets lay. Build the middle first, and then extend it to the heights on either side. Franzysk imagined how eventually such a path would turn the whole route between Sheshul and Petros into one easy walk. However, this turned out to be the only idea thought up in Ialivets that couldn't be realised. Three arches, linked to each other but not with the land – and much higher than the railway bridges at Vorokhta or Deliatyn – hung over the town along one diagonal line, beginning and breaking

off in thin air. On top there was a fragment of wide road. This was where the Unsimple settled.

Franz climbed for a long, long time up a hanging ladder, which swung all the more violently because the snake charmer climbed ahead of him. On top it seemed that the bridge was too narrow, that it would be enough just to stumble and you'd plunge downwards: onto the little roofs, the short streets, the narrow canals, the foam of the trees. But all around lay such beauty, as though in someone else's life. Everything was whitened, other colours didn't exist, even in the faraway sun.

The snow-covered Unsimple smoked pipes and looked out at Farkhaul in the Maramorski Alps beyond the Bila Tysa valley. The conversation was simple – when Anna became a woman, she would become Unsimple. And for the time being they would always be close by.

9   And so the film that Franz completed was similar to a chain of knots.

It looked like this. The whole screen was filled with a multitude of tiny, separate, seething signs. These were all the basic symbols that Franz had managed to discern on the patterns of *pysanky*[1] from all corners of the Carpathians. Due to the variation in size, configuration, colour and speed, this mist of signs resembled an incredible mixture of different insects. One could make out ladders, triangles, half-triangles, triple triangles, forty-triangles, yellow triangles, teeth, seams, cages, infinities, half-infinities, curls, gaps, crosses, scratches, curves, sparkles, stars, warming suns, half-suns, moons, half-moons, sparks, shining moons, moon streets, rainbows, beans, roses, half-roses, acorns, flowers, black eyebrows, corn-ears, heather blossoms,

---

1. *Pysanky* are traditional Ukrainian painted Easter eggs. The complex and intricate patterns on the eggs are made up of many different symbols and elements, each of which has its own name and often its own meaning (*Translator's note*).

pine trees, cucumbers, cloves, periwinkles, oats, orchids, barrels, plums, potatoes, branches, soapwort, horses, sheep, cows, dogs, goats, deer, cockerels, ducks, cuckoos, cranes, whitewings, trout, crows' feet, rams' horns, hares' ears, oxes' eyes, butterflies, bees, snails, spiders, heads, spindles, rakes, brushes, combs, axes, shovels, boats, flasks, grates, chests, girths, straps, knapsacks, keys, beads, kegs, sheepskins, powder horns, umbrellas, pictures, handkerchiefs, laces, bowls, huts, shutters, pillars, troughs, churches, monasteries, bell towers, chapels, twisted sleeves, decorated sleeves, diagonal stripes, needles, little beaks, criss-crosses, symbols toothed, braided and laced, princesses, crooks, curves, dots, frayed, winged, eyed, spidery, flowery, flat and numbered signs, flasks, secrets, cherries, raspberries, flowerpots, sprouts, damselflies, windmills, sledges, hooks, honeycakes.

Slowly the movement of signs gained a certain order – like a powerful wind gathering many lighter ones. The symbols whirled around, a bit like a bath full of water draining out through a small plughole. Then from the hole a chain of signs emerged, tied together here and there by knots. The chain curled itself into a spiral and spun like a centrifuge. From the chaos free symbols flew towards it and arranged themselves in exactly the same order of signs, ever more closely following the turning movement of the first chain. Then both spirals flowed together into the vacuum, merging with each other more and more tightly, and took the shape of the world tree. Calm descended. The tree produced flowers, the petals withered, the ovaries grew into fruit, which swelled, split, and thousands of the very same signs slowly and evenly descended onto the ground, piling up into a mound and losing their form.

10 They waited until Easter 1900 for the premiere. It marked the opening of the cinematograph 'YUNIPERUS', which was built according to one of Anna's sketches. A pastoral message from the young Stanislaviv bishop Andrei Sheptytskyi to his beloved Hutsul brothers was also read out at the ceremony.

11 From that time on the Unsimple really were always nearby. It only seems that Chornohora is empty. In truth, there is really too little space in the Carpathians. For this reason people who live far away from one another are constantly meeting. To say nothing of a small town at the intersection of two ridges.

For a few Dovbush gold pieces the Unsimple bought a small plot on the Market Square and built a small building there. They covered the hut with weirdly painted tiles, so that it came to look just like a stove. In each window they wrote one word: 'NOTARY'. But on the windowsills stood whole rows of different-sized and differently-shaped bottles, so that it could be assumed that NOTARY was just the name of another bar. Lukač somehow saw to it that in just one week the whole roof became covered in moss, and above the doors hung a green awning. Inside, it was sparsely furnished – opposite a small table (with one drawer) on very high legs stood a comfortable armchair, upholstered in canvas.

In the armchair sat the notary himself, smoking one fat cigarette after another, the cigarettes placed in a silver ring soldered onto a long tin rod that was attached to the ceiling. Each cigarette was no longer than half the length of an average woman's hand. The notary kept busy by rolling the next cigarette while smoking the previous one.

While he was still young he had decided somehow to control his own death, and not rely entirely on the unknown. Therefore he wanted to determine, if not the date then, at least, the reason for his death. He settled on cancer of the lungs and began to allow himself to smoke heavily in order to be doomed to such a death.

12 But if someone were to call in, the notary would take the cigarette out of the ring, sit the visitor in his armchair, open the drawer, take out two sweet red or yellow peppers – always fresh and juicy; with one hand he would open a large folding knife which

hung from a strap around his knee and clean out the peppers, which he held in the other hand, then he would ask what kind of spirit to pour – *palenka, rakia, slyvovytsia, bekherivka, tsuika, zubrivka, anisivka, ialivitsivka* or *borovichka* – would fill the two peppers with whatever was chosen, give one pepper to the guest, stand by the table, take a sheet of paper and sharp pencil out of the drawer, raise his improvised cup, say 'God willing!' while looking straight in the visitor's eyes, drink, take a bite of the pepper, immediately pour a second, relight the cigarette (he kept his matches in his trouser pocket right next to his belt, and the striking surface was stuck to one of the legs of the table), he would hold the cigarette in the same hand as his cup and, the pencil in his left, would take a deep draw of smoke, and was ready to listen.

13 The notary was known as the French engineer.

The Unsimple found him in Rakhiv and offered him precisely this job, because he looked modest and heroic at once. He was the sort of man you feel you want to surprise with some extraordinary tale from your own life. And the Unsimple needed as many such stories and tales as possible.

In Rakhiv the French engineer had been enlisting people to go to Brazil, providing genuine tickets for a ship from Genoa. Once he really had been a French engineer. He lived for twenty years in Indochina, developing drainage systems, learning about opium smoking, Thai boxing, butterflies and orchids, Zen. At the same time he wrote articles on ethnology and geopolitics for big European newspapers. Several of his letters were translated by Osyp Shpytko. They were published in the newspaper *Dilo*, with specific emphasis put on the author's connection to the Orlyk family.

The Unsimple visited Kryvorivna and advised Hrushevskyi to bring the French engineer to Lviv. Having passed through Manchuria,

Turkistan, Persia, Georgia, Odesa, Chernivtsi, Stanislaviv, Halych, Rohatyn and Vynnyky he finally arrived and found work in the ethnographic commission of the Shevchenko Scientific Society. He was given funds that had been originally intended for Shukhevych, and set off for Hutsul country. But the experience of the several small wars he had lived through in the course of his life meant that, as a folklorist, he would never betray his principles. The French engineer made a detour to Budapest and managed to obtain a licence that allowed him to enlist people for emigration from the territory of Austria-Hungary.

14 In Ialivets the French engineer dressed the same way every day from 1900 to 1921. (Even after 1914, the French engineer sat in his office listening and noting down everything that various people came to tell him. The storytellers received a decent fee, and the noted-down stories, dreams, insights and insane ideas were analysed by the Unsimple). A broad, white flannel suit, made without a single button, striped white-and-green shirts, unbuttoned at the neck, and cork sandals. Only in winter did he wear a woollen *lizhnyk*, wrapped around his head like a hood.

It was the French engineer who taught Sebastian that self-awareness is found in the soles of the feet, and that one's perception of oneself can be changed by standing differently or on something different.

15 The idea for a whole new type of film was given to Franzysk by the French engineer.

In Ialivets there was a small gallery. Its owner, Loci from Beregszász, was acquainted with talented artists – Munkácsy, Ustyianovych, Kopystynskyi. He introduced Romanchuk to Fedkovych, and for Vodzytska (much later, when she had returned from Paris and her time with Zuloaga) he made a few photo-sketches for 'Girl making pysanky'. He was a close friend of Ivan Trush. Loci told Trush a lot about how plants can regain control of landscapes ruined and abandoned by people. He even took him sketching near Pip Ivan, where trees had been felled. Many years later Trush would return to this theme in his wonderful series 'The Lives of Tree-stumps'. And in the end it was Loci who first took people to Dzembronia, which later became a favourite place for many artists of the Lviv school. And he would regularly send the Didushynskyis Hutsul rarities for their museum.

16 Loci himself painted the same thing his whole life – little wooden cowsheds, a separate one for each cow – on the Shesa plain, the wooden walkways between them and the giant overgrowth of sorrel gradually consuming its own environment.

Although he owned his own gallery, he never displayed his own work. On the other hand he often fell in love with the work of others. He would take his picture-lovers home for a time and live in their presence, carrying them with him from the bedroom to the kitchen, from the kitchen to the study, from the study to the showroom, from the showroom to the bathroom.

Loci's life was defined to a large extent by the picture that was living with him at any given moment.

17 In the gallery some unusual things were practised. Every day, Loci re-hung the pictures, completely changing their dialogues. Often, having chosen a picture one day, the buyers could not recognise it the next morning. The roof of the gallery consisted of a glass reservoir filled with rainwater. Loci changed the lighting of the room by covering different parts of the reservoir with spruce branches. But the most important thing was that the pictures could be borrowed, like books from a library. Loci put together orders from the most expensive hotels himself, according to each individual occasion.

18 Loci was the only person in Ialivets whose vines produced high-quality ripe grapes. His vineyard grew along a path between the house and the gallery. Each time he walked along the path, Loci would pick off at least one cluster of grapes. And so it continued from the appearance of the ovary to the final ripening. Although by September there were only a few dozen clusters left, they were as ripe as the grapes of Tokay, since they could take full benefit from the strength of the vines, which was no longer required by the picked bunches.

Although Franzysk was friends with the gallery owner, even he did not guess that Loci was working for the Unsimple.

19 Once the French engineer told Franz what he had heard from Loci.

Loci had told him how an old man from Teresva had come and asked him to paint a picture in which would be shown what is happening to the left beyond the frame of a scene depicting the battle of Khotyn that he had bought there a year earlier. The old man suspected that from there a cannon would be able to strike directly at the rear-guard of the Ulans, and this thought gave him no peace.

This is precisely where animation is better than painting, said the French engineer.

20 Franzysk came up with a more precise method. He filmed an enlarged reproduction of a famous picture – and this was the second part of the film. For the first and third parts he painted scenes showing fifteen seconds before the scene in the picture, and the same for fifteen seconds after. As a test he used a recent landscape by Trush, *The Dnipro near Kyiv*, although Franz was thinking mainly of Rembrandt's *The Night Watch*. Then he animated several still lifes by the old Dutch masters (although he destroyed all of these except

a Jan van de Velde – the one with the deck of cards, pipe with a long stem and hazelnuts) and the wonderful *A Fight* by Adrian van Ostade (an inn, drunk villagers, women hold back two men with mad looks in their eyes waving knives, everything has been overturned, someone is running away, others have fallen to the ground).

After this he started on paintings of the Cossack Mamai.

Living painting was such a wild success that for every premiere dozens of viewers would travel to Ialivets from all over Central Europe; the films were written about in major journals, and Franz had no time to make more serious films.

21 Even before the Unsimple had discovered the unusual qualities of Anna's dreams, one of Franzysk's ambitions was to make a film that would be based on a dream landscape.

He noticed that the mechanism of dreams is based on nothing other than the unification of the well known according to the principles of an unknown logic – as it could never be in one single landscape. This means that the key to this logic is the unification of landscapes. In this the sequence unification is definitive. When such a landscape is created, it populates itself arbitrarily. And then all the characters will no longer display their natural traits. And – most importantly – the characters will occupy the space totally. Irrational coherence is complete.

22 And also, thought Franz, good dreams are like good prose, with similes taken from different systems of coordinates, refined distinctions of individual details in the flow of a panorama, transparent endlessness of possibility, an unforgettable sensation of presence, simultaneousness of all tropisms, the unrestrainedness of the unexpected and the modest rhetoric of restraint. It's like good marijuana, which doesn't bring with it anything of its own, but

removes that which limits, and transforms the lattice of the proportions of time and distance from a crystallised state to a gas-like one.

23 However, daring to make such a film would be even more difficult than making *The Night Watch*. So in time he even stopped saving dreams for later, enjoying them instead to the full at night.

24 In July 1904 Anna recounted one of her dreams.

I'm standing on the level roof of a long, two-storey building. The building is surrounded by water. The water reaches right up to the top of the first floor. To the top of its high arches. In the water three heads float, and a heron stands. One head swims up under an arch. Another wants to swim out from there. Down the stairs from the window of the second storey walks a naked, tubby man. A dried-up hand protruding from round the corner tries to stop him. I'm also naked. I'm standing on the very edge. My hands raised upwards. Placed together. I'm about to jump from that height into the water. Immediately behind me is a round table. And behind it, a barrel with a jug. At the table sit a monk and a nun, drinking something. Above the table, the barrel, the monk and the nun, a tent is stretched across a dry branch. On the side of the building the semi-sphere of a dome with a chapel at the top has been built. Fire pours from the chimney of the chapel, and a woman looks out of the window. She is looking at me. Far beyond the dome are a wide river, a green forest and high, blue mountains, like ours. On the other side of the building a round tower has been built. On its walls little men have been painted. The little men dance, jump and tumble over. One is taking a book from the sky. Two carry on their shoulders an enormous raspberry on a stick. The top of the tower is crumbling and full of holes. Among the ruins grow little trees and a goat is grazing. The water in front of the building ends at a long island. The island is bare and of red clay. At the end of the island stands a windmill. Beyond the island is more water. Beyond the water, a city. Two towers descend right to the water. Between them is a stone bridge. On the bridge is a huge crowd of people with spears raised above their heads. Some of them stand along the barrier and look across the water in my direction. In one tower branches are burning. Between the towers swim some kind of creatures. A man with a sword and shield is fighting with one of them. Further, beyond the towers, is an empty, sandy place. In the middle of it stands a two-wheeled cart. Further still is the city. Buildings with sharp roofs, a tall church, a wall. And in the distance high mounds, or small, bare, green mountains. On the very horizon is another windmill. To my right, but beyond the water and the island, some figures stand on the shore. With their backs to me. Some sit on horses or on strange creatures. One is in armour and a helmet, another has a hollow tree stump on his head. Between them grows a dried-up tree. Half the tree is covered with a red curtain. In a great crack in the trunk stands a naked woman. On the uppermost branch sits a woodpecker – a very big one. A man is leaning a ladder against the tree. Quite far away behind them on a stone sits a bearded man in a monk's cassock, with a stick in his hand, looking at a book. He looks like my Saint Anthony.

Through the shutters in the round tower, which I already mentioned, I see that behind the tower something important is happening. But I can't make anything out, which really frustrates me. All the same it's really good to be in the middle of all this movement. For a second I look over my shoulder and see a distant fire. It makes the skin on my back and on the back of my legs hot. Somehow it's clear that I have to escape from it into the water. I'm already about to jump, but then I look down and see a length of sharp wire stretched out below. I don't doubt that I can jump beyond it. But I still stand there. My hands are already a little tired, because they're raised the whole time. Suddenly a shadow falls on my back and it gets colder. I look up. Directly above me a sailing ship covered in armour is floating past in the air. I see its underside. It's a flying ship. It flies past. The shadow disappears. Once again it gets hot. Hotter and hotter. I want to take the step. But I see a man with a camera.

He's been hiding the whole time in a dark corner between my building and the tower with the paintings of the little men and the shutters. I don't want him to take my photograph, and I shout at him. The man waves his hands in denial and points at the flying ship. Everything in me feels how interesting this all is. The man hides the camera in the wall. He walks around the tower and disappears behind it. I stand up on my toes. I sway a little, then jump. I see the wire before me. I raise my whole body. I try to fly over it. But my body won't move. I am neither flying nor falling. I start to cough. At great speed I fly straight towards the wire. I hit it with the fingers of my outstretched hands. And with that I woke up.

25 Anna's dream seemed so picturesque to Franzysk that he immediately tried to draw it. Anna corrected the drawing as he drew. When they got to the people on the shore next to the tree and the man with the book behind them, Franz had the impression he'd already seen this painted somewhere. Only the point of view was different. But it was enough for Anna to colour in the drawing with colouring pencils, and Franz recognised Bosch. Without a doubt – *The Temptation of St Anthony*.

In Larousse, Heironymous Bosch was represented by *The Wayfarer* from the collection at El Escorial near Madrid. Anna could not have seen any other reproductions, Franz was sure, he had always been by her side. No one had ever told her about *The Temptation* in her entire life, and Franz was certain he had heard neither mention of it nor allusion to it since the very beginning of her education. That meant that the seeress's prediction had come true – Anna's dreams showed how things could be.

But Franz couldn't let it lie. He ran off to Loci and asked him to order at the first convenient opportunity an album of Bosch's paintings. Franz was prepared to wait a good while, as long as he would eventually be sure that something was going on.

Loci promised to order the album the very next day. And said that he had Bosch in his own library, but only one reproduction – *The Temptation of St. Anthony*.

Anna without hesitation pointed out her naked figure in the upper right-hand corner of the central part of the picture.

When at the very same moment they recognised Unsimple in two of the four main figures walking across the bridge on the left-hand panel of the triptych, Franzysk promised himself he would make that film.

26 This time the work was tougher than it had ever been before. Franzysk was troubled by doubt. He constantly wondered whether he would be able to convey the mood, the colour, the atmosphere, whether he would be able to decode all the secret meanings, whether it was right to show anyone something like this, whether Bosch wouldn't look ridiculous and tasteless, whether it would be a sin to reproduce all this filth and sodomy, whether he would offend the Unsimple, whether he wouldn't call down calamity on Anna, whether he hadn't done someone harm consciously or unconsciously, whether art made any sense, whether he would live to the end of the work, whether something bad might not happen at the showing, whether he would die in suffering, whether he would meet his parents after his death, whether his own Anna was waiting for him there, whether his people would ever be happy, whether there was anything better in the world than our beloved Carpathian mountains, whether it was worth thinking so much, whether it was worth remembering so much, whether it was good to tell everyone all this, whether it was necessary to speak beautifully, whether plants think, whether tomorrow exists, whether the end of the world hadn't happened already sometime

before, whether he would hold out much longer without a woman, whether he wasn't under the control of the devil.

27 The exact answer to the last question would have been the answer to many of the others. Despite the fact that Franz was a devout Greek Catholic, and that in the frequent discussions over gin at the mountain resort he always attacked the Manicheans, the Cathars and the Albigensians with his arguments, and that he feared nothing on earth, for he was convinced of the rectitude of God's plan, despite this the devil appeared to him thrice during work on this film.

28 The first time he did not show himself, but only very laconically showed one of his traits. He was like a magnet.

Franz dreamed that he was lying on the floor. Suddenly, without making a single movement, not even tensing his muscles, he slid along the floor to the wall. Then in the other direction. Then again and again, with intervals, now quickly, now slowly As though he were metal filings on a sheet of paper, and under the paper a magnet was being moved. Once he was even pulled up the wall – lying in the same position – and then delicately lowered to the floor.
After this the devil asked him to follow carefully what would happen. He dragged Franz into the corner. It turned out that his teacher was asleep there. Franz was shoved towards the teacher and immediately pulled back. The teacher, not touching Franz's body and without waking up, slid after him. See, said the devil.

Franz didn't hear the voice, but somehow he knew what the devil had said.

29 In the second and third dreams the devil used different variations of this very same method.
The second dream was the shortest. Franz was standing in the street

in Ialivets (the place was real, he knew it well). He was waiting for his Anna, who had already appeared at the end of the street. Suddenly Beda's armoured car drove up to him. Beda looked out through the top hatch and said that he had brought someone with whom they would now go and drink gin. From the side door a fellow appeared and came up to Franz. Anna was getting closer. The fellow stood with his back to Anna and the car. He took a bottle from his inside pocket, pulled out the cork and offered the bottle to Franz. And now it all happened. In the few seconds it took Anna and Beda to reach them Franz had time to see several thousand different faces pass over the place where the fellow's face should have been, several hundred waistcoats under his unbuttoned jacket, several dozen forms of bottle and more than a dozen shades of drink. When the fellow and Franz were no longer alone the kaleidoscope stopped. The fellow smiled, Anna and Beda smiled. Franz drank first. The taste reminded him of greengages. He passed the bottle to Beda, and Beda passed it to the fellow (Beda hadn't actually introduced them to one another). When it came to Anna's turn, Franz for some reason blurted out that she didn't drink. Nobody, apart from Anna, was surprised, and nobody insisted. And Franz discreetly but tightly squeezed her finger. He already knew who this was.

30 After the third dream Franz went to the high bridge and told the Unsimple about Bosch. 'In the tower after all,' said the hill wanderer. Franz asked whether he should show anyone the now completed film. That depends entirely on your wishes, answered the Unsimple. Although think about it, maybe it's not right to show our faces in the place where you dreamed all this up. But for now go home and look after Anna, we must wander a little among the worlds, but soon she'll be a woman and will know where to find us, said the *bai*-maker.

31 At home Franz burned the drawing that depicted Anna's dream.

'In order to be happy,' he told Anna, 'you have to live without secrets, and of others know only what you can tell under torture.'

He was very afraid that the Unsimple might sooner or later come for the film, and so told Anna never to mention its existence. But if someone were to want to find something out using torture, then she should tell them everything they wanted straight away. Not try to fool them, but tell the truth. Therefore you must know that I've destroyed everything.

Franz packed the film into his tobacco pouch and went outside the town to burn it, throw it into a ravine or into a torrent. On the way he thought: no matter how they torture her, Anna will tell the truth – there is no film. It's paradoxical, but that will be the only truth the torturers won't believe, and the torture won't stop.

In that case it's a shame to destroy the film. Maybe it will come in useful someday. Let someone find it who will watch it, analyse it, think hard about it and understand what these Unsimple are about, with their wanderings around the world. For it always gradually comes to light, how everything and everyone in the world are connected with everything and everyone else – by paths, of which there are no more than four.

32 Franzysk went into a beech forest in which every tree had a hollow under its roots. Around his eyes he wrapped a strip of cloth taken from a long gown, so that he could see only where he was standing, and began to run blindly about the forest. Several times he collided with a tree, but it was all right, because his eyes were protected. He ran uphill and downhill, until inside his hood all the sounds of the world were replaced by the sound of wheezing from the depths of his lungs. It was only then that he stopped and, without opening his eyes, reached out, found a tree, found the hollow between the roots and stuffed the pouch with the film inside into the hole, deeper

in than one-and-a-half forearms. And then he slowly made his way out of the forest. In these places this is easy to do without looking. You have to go upwards, following the slope of the ground. At the top Franz took off the ice-covered sleeve and looked at the forest. All the trees were identical and unfamiliar, between them curled endless intertwined lines of footprints, and his eyes hurt from the shameless light of the moon.

33 Of course, it was winter. Of course – snow was falling. You could spin round, catching the snowflakes in your dry mouth.

34 At home Franzysk couldn't smell his daughter. He thought he really was living after the end of the world, which had happened not long ago. In the house he could hear only the flow of water deep in the pipes, the contraction of the metal in the doors of the cold stove, the ultrasonic vibrations of the panes of glass in the windows, it smelled of sulphur and coal – the pressure was changing.

Franzysk ventured to glance out through the open doors of the balcony. The blanket spread out in the garden looked like a painful stain. On the blanket slept a little girl, shivering from the cold, who had never yet fallen asleep without her father. In order for a draught to be created, a little time is necessary. So it began to smell of Anna after almost a minute. Franzysk felt that he didn't want her to become a woman.

35 After that night the Unsimple really did leave Ialivets, somehow managing to throw their rope ladder back up onto the viaduct. The French engineer remained; he didn't even stop his work for a day. Franzysk stopped making animations. Now he, together with Anna and the Serb Lukač, who marked all his movements around the world by planting forests, occupied themselves with improving the town. He drank a little (mostly he would draw an equator of full

shotglasses across a circular table in the bar, and would go nowhere until he'd emptied the whole row), but refused all gin-based remedies that were on offer at the resort.

He built himself an orangery where he cultivated tropical plants. He observed the changing resemblances of the offspring of Lukač the dog, whom he had to kill in the orangery. Sometimes he would take an axe in each hand and run like that all the way to Menchil. From there he would bring back fresh *bryndza* cheese, slinging an axe with round wooden containers fastened to each end, like a yoke with buckets, across his shoulders. He gave interviews reluctantly, but conscientiously. He usually insisted that he made different films in order to live in different ways.

36 In 1910, the deputies of the Vienna parliament Mykola Lahodynskyi and Vasyl Stefanyk made a special visit to Ialivets with the aim of persuading Franzysk to return to his work. Franzysk did not argue but promised nothing. He received the deputies not at home but in the CPT hotel, which stood for Cheremosh, Prut, Tysa.

Lahodynskyi later recalled how Franzysk Petroskyi said that a Ukrainian state would be possible only when the Carpathian vector became the basis of its geopolitics, Carpathian cosmogony the model for its ideology, and the Carpathians themselves a nature reserve (Franz did not especially believe in what he said, for he hated the Hutsul desire to cut down in the course of their lives as much forest as possible, and the Hutsuls' failure to understand that there was now more and more rubbish that could not just be thrown away into water).

37 As for Stefanyk, he said more to Franzysk's Vienna acquaintances. 'Every human being,' so said Franz, 'can in their lifetime make a book. I say a book, although we began talking about films. Every human, but only one book. Those who think they have

written many books are mistaken – they are always working on the same thing. You cannot escape your own book, no matter what you change. You can imitate, but not create. Your single book is defined by your timbre, intonation, articulation. Fate is a way of speaking. Although there is an infinity of books in the world, the number of genuinely good ones is finite. It must be finite, and there must be an infinity. This is what plants teach us. If the number of good books were not finite, the world would stop or take to drink. I've written my book. I don't know whether it is good or not, but I've written it. And it's like this: it's already meaningless whether I've finished it or not finished it, whether I rewrote it or merely intended to. Your book is just the same whether it's one page or whether its volumes fill a whole bookshelf. The voice exists – that's enough. Plots are necessary for your own curiosity. Plots are neither invented nor do they disappear. They simply are. They can only be forgotten. All that I've learned and memorised in my life consists of a few landscapes, which signified the joy of thinking; a few smells, which were emotions; a few movements, which adorned themselves in feelings; a few things, objects, which were the embodiment of culture, history, sufferings; many plants, which were access to beauty, wisdom and to all that, in comparison with which we simply do not exist in the world. And many, many intonations. Unique, similar intonations, the significance of which I do not know. Perhaps they will help us recognise each other in the place where nothing but the voice remains.'

38 Stefanyk was also pleased when, after Lahodynskyi had gone to rest, they began to call each other all sorts of different names – you blind bat, you free-loader, you four-eyes, you brat, you whimperer, you mumbler, you stutterer, you cock-eye, you bandit, you ne'er-do-well, you intriguer, you layabout, you rascal, you glass-peddler, you newcomer, you playboy, you nouveau-riche, you low-lander, you highlander, you Bukovinian, you Boiko, you Lemko, you Hutsul – and then fell asleep.

39 Two years previously Franzysk had first taken Anna to the place from which he had returned alone fifteen years earlier. Anna never managed to visit the place again even once. Nevertheless, this was the beginning of the only tradition their family had.

In autumn 1913, Anna still was not yet a woman. And at around that time the birds flew over Ialivets on their way to Africa. Franzysk felt it: a little longer, and he would have to cry. The most important things don't happen out of your own will, he thought, and asked Anna to make a large pot of coffee and squeeze the juice from four grapefruits the size of small pumpkins.

Franzysk realised that he couldn't, when he closed his eyes, exactly recall the outlines of all the surrounding mountains, just as before he had begun to forget all the unforgettable women's breasts that he had known. For this reason he had to climb up onto the cliff in order to look at what he had loved so much. And he wanted to make sure, before leaving on his walk, that the coffee and grapefruit juice would be waiting for him when he returned.

40 He returned home, having re-familiarised himself with all the peaks, together with Sebastian. Franz proposed that he try living a while in Ialivets. Anna made up another bed in the spare room. For some reason she had had the second key to the room since morning.

Franzysk felt that Anna's scent had stopped being a child's, and that the Unsimple might come very soon, because the blood of the guest, like an airborne disease, had begun to mix in the air with the blood of the women of his kind already.

Sebastian wanted to sleep so much that he accepted with gratitude Franz's invitation to live a while in Ialivets.

And Anna thought to herself that it would be hard for Sebastian, trying all the time to be friend to parent and husband to daughter.

Naked vine branches tapped on the window above the bed. Sebastian noticed that the rhythm of their taps could serve as an anemometer.

ISOBAR PRESS — *English writing from Japan*
http://isobarpress.com

Recent books: *A Draft Will*, Peter Robinson's book of prose poems and memoirs; *Neck of the Woods*, Peter Makin's collected poems; *One More Civil Gesture*, C. E. J. Simons's striking collection of formally inventive verse; *Beethoven's Dream*, the completion of Eric Selland's modernist *haibun* trilogy; *World Without*, a gathering of recent work by Paul Rossiter; and *Dreaming of Zeus*, Lesley Hardy's vivid verse portraits of musicians, Ohio Presbyterians, Greek gods and medieval philosophers.

AVAILABLE FROM THE LRB BOOKSHOP & AMAZON

My sleep is fitful and disturbed.

My hands and feet are usually warm enough.

I have numbness in one or more regions of my skin.

A Minister can cure diseases by praying and putting his hand on your head.

I sometimes tease animals.

I am afraid of losing my mind.

Sometimes I am strongly affected by the personal articles of others such as shoes, gloves, etc., so that I want to handle or steal them though I have no use for them.

At times I feel like smashing things.

I have never felt better in my life than I do now.

I dream frequently about things that are best kept to myself.

I sweat very easily even on a cool day.

I do not blame a person for taking advantage of someone who lays himself open to it.

It makes me feel like a failure when I hear of the success of someone I know well.

I am embarrassed by dirty stories.

I try to remember good stories to pass them on to other people.

Someone has been trying to rob me.

I have had no difficulty starting or holding my urine.

I enjoy gambling for small stakes.

I should like to belong to several clubs or lodges.

I like to talk about sex.

Statements from a psycho-diagnostic test developed in the USA in the 1940s. Subjects were asked to respond, true, false or cannot say.

SALIM BARAKAT

from *The Caves of Hydrahodahose*

translated from the Arabic by Sawad Hussain

Recent Syrian literature reflects the chaos that has overtaken the country; war, the corrupted ruling regime and life as a refugee are, understandably, key leitmotifs. Even if you go back to the early 2000s – before the explosion of the conflict – the trend was to show real life, or at least to draw from it quite heavily: life in the countryside or the city; unrequited love; women fighting societal restraints. Uniquely, Salim Barakat's novel The Caves of Hydrahodahose *avoids falling into step with any of these narrative standards.* The Caves of Hydrahodahose *emerges from the loom of magical realism, from where it unrolls an entirely new world far removed from our own. Centaurs are the protagonists, dreams are more valuable than money and cucumber butter is a breakfast staple. Although we see reflections of our reality in the social hierarchies, in the characters' attempts to preserve their history, and in the temptations and corrupting effects of power, the manner in which Barakat depicts each is unlike any other Arabic writing I have come across.*

One could argue that, in the greater sphere of Arabic literature, novelists such Fadhil al-Azzawi (Iraq), Ibrahim Al-Kuni (Libya) and Emile Habiby (Lebanon) also incorporate elements of magical realism into their work. Closer to Barakat's approach is the widely celebrated short story pioneer, Zakaria Tamer, who also draws on the palette of magical realism. However, whereas these authors paint recognisably magical realist strokes across their pages, Barakat dunks his entire novel in the paint box: every page is dripping wet with the fantastical.

Barakat is a revolutionary stylist. The Caves of Hydrahodahose *is crafted in his own 'prosetical' style – an idiosyncratic mash-up of prose and poetry – and marks a high point of this technique within Barakat's career as a writer and poet. Thus he has, incidentally, made it exceptionally difficult not only to translate his novel, but also for (even Arab) readers to understand it. Barakat admits that this is wholly intentional; he insists that not everything needs to be interpreted or picked apart – as in poetry, some images or constructions should just be. Although daunting to both reader and translator, this unusual style elevates the novel to an exalted status within Arabic literature.* The Caves of Hydrahodahose *marks a new adventure on the high seas of storytelling.*

— S.H.

Marcia Lynx Qualey: BARAKAT'S RULES

Salim Barakat wears his 'rain and sweat-soaked vest' in a Swedish exile, far from his native Syria. As Mahmoud Darwish writes in the poem 'In Skogås,' Barakat is living in the isolation 'chosen for him by the artful winds of fate.'

It's in this cold, isolated north where Barakat invents a new Arabic literature. To open one of his novels is to be dis-oriented, to be thrown into an unfamiliar world where both word and image are bent to the author's will.

Born in 1951 in a Kurdish region of Syria, Barakat first moulded the Arabic language to fit the stories of his Kurdish boyhood. Barakat came to the Syrian Arabic writing scene in a time of ferment, when Adonis and Muhammad al-Maghut had been reinventing poetry while Zakariya Tamer worked on the short story, fusing oral and written traditions. Magical realism and science fiction found an early hold in Syria. Novelists took up history and allegory to shed light on the all-consuming state. Censorship forced many of them into different exiles.

Barakat, who writes both poetry and prose, didn't just critique the world around him. Instead, he re-invented it. His experiments began with the 'unfinished' memoir of his childhood and adolescence, al-Jundub al-Hadidi (The Iron Grasshopper). *In it, he re-fashioned the Arabic language, violating the boundaries between poetry and prose. He drew on Arabic classics in order to take words and phrases, put them into a new context, and hammer out new meanings for them, much as his friend Darwish would do in his prose works.*

As Barakat moved into novel-writing, he merged narrative, folk reality and classical poetry. His novels describe babies who grow to adulthood in a matter of hours, anthropomorphised trees and cave-dwelling centaurs. It takes a reader time to adjust her view to that of Barakat's world; at first it can be dizzying. To enter one of his books is to learn a new grammar that, after a few pages, seems spookily familiar.

In his poem Darwish paints an affectionate portrait of Barakat living in his remote exile south of Stockholm. This Barakat gives Kurdish names to the many birds of the forest as he lives and writes far from the jealousies of other writers. In the following section, translated by Catherine Cobham, the Syrian writer is cooking:

To kindle the desire between the eater and the eaten, he selects hot, pungent spices, special mushrooms to enhance the word play, and Shiraz wine to stimulate the poet's inclination to rejoice and sing in the autumn of exile. He drags his little cart through the forest, accompanied by the birds of the north who recognise him from his rain and sweat-soaked vest. Nobody but a Kurd like him would brave the Baltic climate.

Barakat has been somewhat marginalised by the new Arabic-novel prize scene with its focus on fast-paced readability. What's more, the difficulty of translating (and marketing) his worlds in other languages has largely kept him off the global circuit. But, as the great modernist poet Adonis is credited with saying, 'the Arabic language is in Salim Barakat's pocket.'

Thunderbolt in the Great Cave

Thayouni brushed a kohl-soaked quill over his eyes. He asked his wife to dismiss the two sister beauticians, Safinos and Rosina, should they come in early that morning. When they duly arrived, Aniksamida sent them away. 'The prince is occupied today with addressing the all-seeing black crystal,' she said.

With assistance from his wife, Thayouni removed his golden horseshoes using iron pliers and replaced them with lead ones. He put on a grey, burnous-like cloak: it was long, loose and hooded. He hooked his arms into the hoops of his holster belt, from which two regular steel daggers hung, suspended beneath his armpits. 'How do I look, Hodahose princess?' he inquired of his wife. She shook her head disapprovingly. 'What do you want of the Hydrahodahose people? Your idea is a confused one, Hodahose prince,' she determined.

Examining her, Thayouni looked like a gooseherd on the yellow sand-covered banks of the Sitam River. 'If I come back with nothing, that would be laughable. Make sure that no one follows me. I'll leave, concealed in my hooded cloak, by the passage that runs between the ovens and leads up to the door of the cave of provisions. Make sure the cooks and those kneading dough in the troughs are fully engrossed in their work.'

His lead horseshoes pounded the cave's earthen ground, his hoofbeats muffled. Since Thayouni had exhausted the dreams of his loyal cadre and the Great Cave's dignitaries, he decreed that those of the masses be brought to him. Every pair that held equal parts of the same dream was to come to his breakfast, where he would hungrily listen to them as they narrated what their sleep had captured of their imaginations, what kinds of images it had retained and which elements of reality had played a part. During those first nineteen mornings, Thayouni's heart quaked. Not a soul revealed his dreams. Those who had been brought by messengers stood silent next to his stone slab of a dining table. A few responded, 'We revere Colour. The dream is one of its many secrets. We will not insult Colour.'

For nineteen mornings, tails were cut amidst the statues of the stone gardens. Flies of shame hovered above the wounds that would not heal except in death: those whose tails had been chopped off committed suicide with their own daggers, each releasing a desolate final moan.

In one of the caves, replete with breathings from the corn-covered plains, middle-aged warriors gathered by unspoken agreement with dignitaries fortunate enough to enjoy keen foresight. 'Let us expand our minds during this trying time for our intellects,' they agreed. They chose a messenger to send to Kaydromi, the seer. 'Let the prince give us a few days of respite while we solve the problem at hand,' they advised one another.

After intoning a stormy chant for wind cleansed with the scent of nine leopards, Kaydromi sent them an authoritative word: 'Take your time. Though it is short.' But the wind, which revealed the plains and some of the arrangements conspiring, sprinkled fire on the swelling problem, like sesame seeds on bread loaves. The wise men were divided amongst themselves. Some commanded those who wanted to rebel not to reveal their dreams. Some considered revealing them, saying, 'We don't want more tails cut off. If the god Colour could forgive the wind, then he, the prince, can forgive as well.' The extremists ignored the chaos. 'We'll see how far this goes,' they declared defiantly.

The wind returned to play over the loaves of unrest, scattering the sesame seeds of panic even further. Whenever the sages fetched a pair of Hodahose to send to the Great Cave, they found that they had had no dreams. They examined hundreds and found that they were not dreaming. The sages urged the common Hodahose to keep their eyes shut night and day, in the hope that if the empty images, which had been reduced to dry straw, were lit by a merciful spark, this would ignite the fire of Colour and bring back images brim-full of it.

The wise men trembled. They realised that they themselves also were not dreaming. Kaydromi's patience ran out. 'The prince chewed his own heart up with pickled pumpkin flowers. He no longer has a heart. Now he will devour yours.' Kaydromi sent the wise men this threat etched into a woody stalk and tied to the leg of a pigeon, which soared across the vast pearl millet field between his cave and that of the middle-aged warrior Nisyano. Nisyano gathered the grief of his imagination between his palms like water, and proceeded to the Fiflafidhi cave.

'Look Hodahose Anistomis, look at the water in my hands,' Nisyano said.

Anistomis didn't see any water in his hands, but she played along and pretended to see this water of many reflections, so that the grave master warrior would be satisfied.

'What do you see?' he asked her.

She responded, 'I see your imagination, Hodahose Nisyano.'

'Yes, these drawings on your cave wall are all that continue to dream; they alone possess dreams today in the land of Hydrahodahose, Anistomis,' he murmured, his tongue scorched by the words.

As if Anistomis's heart was winged, its feathers shuddered. 'What's going on, Nisyano?'

'No one is dreaming, and the prince is waiting for those images that the deity Colour grants to people in the depths of their sleep. From your knowledge of these majestic walls do you have a solution?' he asked, shocked at all that was unfolding before him.

Anistomis shifted her gaze from him to those restoring the columns up above the high scaffolding. She placed her hand on her horn and, after a moment of silence, said, 'I have some sort of knowledge of the wall that is in *here*,' and, gesturing to her forehead, 'a different kind of engraved wall, Nisyano.'

Nisyano's eyes sparkled, in the midst of his yellowing face. His features grew animated. 'Show me the engravings of your imagination, Anistomis.'

'Seeking refuge, they made up dreams, and took them to the prince's breakfast like buffalo buttermilk,' the Fiflafidhi guardian mused.

Nisyano neighed, perplexed. 'How blind our imaginations are! How did we miss this?'

Nisyano carried some cucumber butter to the wise men's breakfast in a cave a short distance beyond the pearl millet plain. The men breathed as if with new lungs. 'Every pair has only tonight to create a dream that will re-enchant the prince's morning. Come on now, show the prince all of Colour's crystals, all that has been stored in the holds of the Hodahose existence,' they said.

Every morning Thayouni devoted himself to listening to a pair of the Hodahose populace, cultivating their one dream with their two tongues; rows sowed in the field of his breakfast. At times he was cheered by their antics and their contradictions. At others, he grew depressed with the misery of their visions. Sometimes he meditated on enigmatic signs in the events described. Sometimes he grew angry at the insolence of their meanings. Sometimes he guffawed at the wildness of the stories until unripe peach vinegar dribbled from the corners of his mouth onto his beard. He stopped some from completing the narration of their dreams altogether, simply out of dislike for their beginnings.

Everything seemed as it should be until the day Katisyas and Sinko, the orphan twins, came to see the prince. Their long red hair reached down their backs and their faces were painted yellow. The prince waited for them to speak but they remained silent. 'What is with you two?' said Aksiyanos. The twins fidgeted. They exchanged agonised glances. 'You can't make me,' said Katisyas, urging on his brother. Sinko responded, 'Not me, *you* first.' Then they spoke in unison, with one tongue, 'Oh prince, we don't dream any more. The dreams that everyone else has been bringing to you . . . they were forced to concoct them.'

Silence cast its net over the assembly, ensnaring all who were seated there. Aksiyanos, the prince's brother, shot up, confused, rousing around him invisible flies of anger. 'Who fabricated these dreams for the people in Hydrahodahose, you wretches?'

'No one. They made them up on their own,' they responded.

Kaydromi got up, stupefied. 'Who trained them?' he demanded. The twins shook their heads: 'No one.'

The seer flared up. His two long moustaches tied by their ends to his ears came loose. Now they hung limp like two snakes down either side of his face.

'Do you know what awaits you two? Your tails will be torn off! You're hiding something,' he bellowed. The prince slowly rose. He whinnied in an obscure tone. Then he spoke, 'No. No one's tail will be cut off. Go on you two.'

The twins retreated and, led by the guide, left the cave all set for breakfast.

Thayouni paced around the long stone slab of a table, overflowing with vegetables soaked in the dawn of Hydrahodahose. 'Did you hear what those two said? The commoners are now able to conjure up our deity Colour whenever they please. They no longer need to wait for Colour to shine upon their dreams, to weave dreams for them out of an imageless haze. They have forced a crack in the gateway there,' he gestured to nowhere in particular in the direction of the ceiling.

That evening, Thayouni revealed to his wife Aniksamida his desire to roam alone among the Hydrahodahose caves. 'I'll leave tomorrow afternoon, in disguise,' he said. He remained at her side as she went back to distributing mirrors with wooden frames onto the protruding ledges of the cave, which was already decked with jewellery and golden vessels. 'Do you think, princess, that those loyal to me and the dignitaries of the Great Cave . . . were also making up the dreams they recounted? If that's the case, then most likely we're the only couple to have shared their halved dreams publicly in our land of Hydrahodahose.'

A mirror fell from Aniksamida's hands. The shards scattered. She nickered angrily. Thayouni approached her. He embraced her shoulders with his arm, leaning into her. 'Look, there are several princesses and princes in the shards,' he said as he contemplated their distributed images in the shattered mirror. He whinnied a whinny laced with recognition. 'I swear by the mirror that I smell the scent of rebellion in Hydrahodahose.'

The rumbling of thunder flooded the Great Cave's entrances. A pigeon ventured in from a narrow window high in the ceiling. It hovered a little before flying out through the same narrow gap.

Azinun

The walls of the great cave pitched to and fro like dizzy, light-headed birds in Aniksamida's eyes. A blade of salt flayed the outer skin of her liver. 'Where's the prince?' she inquired in a thin voice, her throat clogged with panic.

Kaydromi, the seer of the mills, and Aksiyanos, the prince's brother, delivered her an ember of ruinous news. 'We came across Taitona's corpse close to the Saydayn Lake. No sign of the prince.' It was noon of the third day after Thayouni had set out in disguise to wander among the Hydrahodahose caves. The princess had deceived the prince's loyal cohort and the dignitaries of the Great Cave's administration by saying that he had disappeared suffering from a momentary bout of nausea and foul temper. Just as she had deceived her daughters that their father was in one of his customary periods of solitude in his observatory, whose yellow rock walls shot upwards above the cave of the mills. From there, up above, he would examine the lines of the plains inscribed with the god Colour's warm breaths on the mirrors of the horizon and of the sky. But the news of Taitona's murder, his slaughter, his slit throat, stunned Aniksamida and rocked her bones. 'Both of you, send out guards in all directions. Plough the soil of Hydrahodahose, and its clouds, with our soldier's hooves. Find him,' she moaned, her voice subdued.

'Princess, you're right to conceal the prince's disappearance until our minds arrive at what we should do. Aksiyanos and I will rake the land from top to bottom on our own,' Kaydromi assured her. He whinnied as a cloud of trickery went through his heart. His moustache quivered. 'I'll find a temporary way out, Hodahose princess. The inspiration of Colour has touched me.' He turned, seeking someone who would help him. 'Who will bring me the astronomer Medaris?'

In a corner of the stone gardens, close to the statue of a bull with a fish's head, Kaydromi and Aksiyanos met Medaris the astronomer. Two individuals wearing yellow half masks accompanied him – the well-known veiling of those from the Cave of Pigeons. They delivered him and retreated. The three now alone conversed in astronomical terminology: rotation, foci and sequencing. They exchanged their estimations of the air's conditions and its sixteen dispositions, and then they fell silent. Medaris waited for the seed of meaning's fall into the soil of his knowledge, the seed that had been brought along for his sake. Kaydromi neighed, 'You told me once that you saw a poet who resembled the prince, Medaris. Why don't you bring him to us? We'll meet you here in the afternoon.'

Medaris contemplated the invisible seed in the words of the seer, words arranged in the pattern of clouds. 'Azinun?' He stammered. 'You both want Azinun the poet? I can't promise you that I'll have him here by the afternoon. More likely by sunset. Around dusk I can search for him in the many taverns in the Caves of Sand.'

In the same corner of the stone gardens – under the brightness of nine torches held by those wearing the yellow half masks – Kaydromi, Aksiyanos, Medaris and Azinun convened. The seer and the prince's brother were taken aback by the uncanny resemblance between Thayouni and Azinun. Aksiyanos hastily removed his cloak and dropped it over Azinun's head, to keep his features veiled. 'I'm grateful to you, Medaris. We will see you tomorrow,' said the seer, and Medaris understood the sign. He wished them all a night pressed from the grapes of the deity Colour, and good health granted by Colour, and then bid them farewell.

The three entered through the winding corridor leading from the back of the Great Cave to the foyer of the ovens. The guards surrounding the sky-high observatory posts on either side of the entrance did not pay any heed to the stranger they saw in the company of the seer and the prince's brother, who led him amidst the relentless movement of the labourers and chefs to the Cave of Provisions. This was a cave infused with the boundless aroma of spices, herbs and vinegar that would complement the taste of any food, and of smoked birds, cheeses, dried fruits. All of this mixed with the frantic breathing of bakers luring the female kneaders to the side wine galleries, where female body parts would rekindle consciousness in male body parts, and the male in the female counterparts.

In a shaded niche behind a wall of corncobs, Aksiyanos and Azinun sat silently. Kaydromi left them. After a while he came back with Aniksamida in tow, now wearing her own veil. The seated pair stood up. The princess approached Azinun, reached out a hand and drew the veil from his head. Astonished, her heart convulsed. She whinnied forcefully. '*How?* How has Colour been able to piece you, your face, together into the spitting image of Thayouni? Tell me, strange Hodahose, that you're not the prince,' said Aniksamida, and her trembling voice echoed her amazement. Azinun chuckled. 'I can hear in this cave someone singing of waves, and I don't like waves. How can there be a prince who doesn't like waves, oh Hodahose . . . ?' Aksiyanos struck Azinun's hooves with his own. 'She's the *princess*,' he hissed.

Azinun's tongue stuck to the walls of his throat as his imagination crumbled.

'Put your veil back. Drape it over your face as low as you can,' said Aniksamida to the poet. After covering her head with her own veil, she instructed, 'Let's go to the cave of the beauticians Safinos and Rosina.' She advanced a few steps then halted. Wheeling round to Azinun, she said, 'Don't talk to anyone. Be silent.' She went on then stopped once more: 'Be withdrawn.'

Kaydromi asked the princess, 'What should we do about his voice?' She replied, 'Let him tell whoever asks that he's fed up with his voice, and is training to give himself a new one. Tell him that, Hodahose seer.'

A gathering of wives of the Great Cave's dignitaries was clustered, each waiting her turn to enter the beauticians' courtyard with its five wide steps. Each wife would ascend and sit atop the bench in the courtyard, ready for the standing beautician, enabling her to re-tint her face with the dyes of a privileged life. There were six benches apart from those for the customers: two for the two sister beauticians' tools and four others for their assistants. All the female Hodahose stood when the princess entered. Aniksamida beckoned to Rosina, and the dazzling white female hurried to her. Her shield of beads shook with the bouncing of her breasts.

'Haven't you a hidden corner, Hodahose Rosina, to hide us away from prying eyes?' inquired the princess.

'The Cave of Dyes beneath this cave,' answered Rosina. 'We can go down to it by the nine steps at the first turn that leads to the courtyard of the Beautification Cave, Princess.'

Glass vessels. Woven sacks small and large. Clay and brick plates full of paints in the niches bored into the cave's walls. Dried petals, stalks and stone blocks all in baskets. Small troughs. Oils in vials. Smells which one could touch but not smell. Tints one could smell but not touch. This was the state of the Cave of Dyes that Aniksamida, Kaydromi, Rosina, Azinun and Aksiyanos descended into by way of the nine steps. A cave with corners, arched hollows, four thick columns and two deep-set windows lit up by a faint light. With a stone flint Rosina lit the large copper lamp's wick. The shadows argued back and forth a little, then made peace.

Aniksamida drew the veil from Azinun's head. Rosina stammered from the gale of Thayouni's image on her mind. She controlled herself. 'Praise be to Colour for your health, oh Hodahose prince.' Azinun's eyes widened at her voice. Reality was narrowed within his imagination. He did not speak. He remembered to be gruff, so he frowned.

'His beard has grown a bit, Rosina. Trim it back to its usual size, and increase the pigment at his temples,' instructed Aniksamida. Rosina hastened to her instruments and potions. She tossed her tail forcefully to shake off the contentious questions that clung to her white skin like dog fleas: Why had the prince come to the Beautification Cave? His clothes were not of a fabric known in the Great Cave. His two daggers were rather ordinary. There was none of the usual clank to his horseshoes. An unusual, stifled mirth glittered in his eyes despite his grimness. Her breasts rose and fell under the shield of beads on her chest as she turned round, taking what she needed to groom the prince.

Azinun's face emerged from Rosina's hands an even closer likeness to Thayouni than ever.

In another corner of the Great Cave, Azinun summoned up the left-behind shadows of Thayouni's being: his horseshoes, his daggers, his yellow cloak, the thin golden rope around his head and the precise movement of his left hand's fingertips – the way in which he fluttered them like a butterfly if he wanted more of anything. When he attended the first meeting with his daughters, he was preceded by a loud whinny from his attendants announcing that he would be using another voice – a voice that wasn't concerned, a little chatty, swinging between desire and its opposite. He lovingly stroked their heads – just as the princess had dictated – and he allowed their feathered tiaras to drop from their curls. He heard their names from Aniksamida's mouth as she deliberately distanced them from him, one by one. 'Be careful of his cold,' she cautioned. But they looked deep into his eyes, waiting as a cat does for a mouse. They dared to tease him more than ever before. They yanked his tail and touched his daggers.

'Chaos is the original state of things.' These were the words of Azinun posing as Thayouni in the assembly of his loyal cadre and the notables of the Great Cave's administration. 'Chaos is salvation,' he declared from the stone bench on which he sat at the heart of the hall. Aksiyanos sat next to him, deliberately. Whenever a Hodahose creature spoke to Azinun, Aksiyanos announced the name of whoever was speaking and his rank in a booming voice. Aksiyanos would greet them or ask them a question to allow Azinun some time to store the name in the water of his imagination, and in his eyes, the water of images.

'Complete, deep: that is chaos. The system of chaos is a violation of the sacredness of origins, and an insult to the characteristics of creation.' It did not matter that the words Azinun tossed out were swathed in obvious uselessness.

His eyes made those who were seated anxious. Two eyes trapping faces like the gold-plated nets used to catch quail by the people of the fields. How did the prince come back with those two eyes after his disappearance of a mere few days? His loyal cadre and the dignitaries of his administration most likely asked themselves this as they floundered in the nets like butterflies, as if Azinun had stormed their depths.

'The centre is an error in estimation. A sea of emptiness is the centre of oneself. Every sea is a block of conflicting dimensions. There is no balance except in chaos.' Words that did not interest those surrounding Azinun. And he himself was throwing them around as if he had heard them from someone else, luring the assembly into a state of distraction. Though whenever he looked at Anistomis, he would stop interpreting the meaning of chaos. His imagination spun around Anistomis like a dreaming shadow on the face of a dreamer. He breathed in Anistomis from the bewitched branches of eternity . . .

'Every bone in my body is a heart. Every muscle a lung. Every nerve, a soul.'

Aksiyanos had called her by her nickname, Empress of Fiflafidhi. Age-old drawings had engraved names of confusing meanings on clouds as if they were metal. 'How many times have I visited Fiflafidhi?' he asked of her. 'You have never visited Fiflafidhi, Hodahose prince.'

Azinun pounded his chest with his hand: 'I will bring Fiflafidhi Cave to the Great Cave, and carry the Great Cave to Fiflafidhi.'

Aksiyanos was annoyed. Kaydromi neighed.

Aniksamida flapped her fan in front of her face, her thoughts returning to the evening when the prince had divulged his desire to go out into the Hydrahodahose squares and markets in disguise. She could not stand such an agonising thought. She had immediately dispatched the fat cook Kirno the eunuch to Kaydromi the seer. 'The prince will leave on his own tomorrow. Allow him to be followed by whomever you trust from the strongest of the guards of the mills; don't let the prince be aware of this.'

Taitona had observed the prince's exit from the door of the Cave of Provisions, tucked away behind the fruit carts coming in from the fields of the blue Touman River. He had followed him, hooves wrapped in thick buffalo-skin slippers, as is customary for those who do not own horseshoes. He had followed him with mute steps, wary steps, neither recklessly loud nor carelessly calm.

A FEW FACTS about Happen*Stance* Press

- Based in Scotland. Small.
- Publishing poetry since 2005. Lots.
- Flourishes because of its reader-subscribers & excellent poets. All ages and sizes.
- Likes plain-speaking & a singing line.
- Has editor who edits.
- Submission 'windows' in July & December.
- Must sell books in order to make more.

Do buy one. Or, even better—subscribe.

www.happenstancepress.com

BLOWING OUT AN EGG
aged 12

It was a ritual exercise in care—
to blow out a finch's or blue tit's egg,
transforming the patterned container
of life
into the prize itself. First,
the pin-pricked hole in each end, then
holding it poised to your lips
with nail-bitten fingers and thumbs
like a miniature musical instrument
you were trying to gentle a note from,
pursing your mouth with precise
   pressure
to start the albumen's gossamer
lengthening into the toilet bowl. And
   after,
if the egg was fresh as it should be,
the pumping gold of what would now
be no singing bird, in small rich gouts
sinking through the water to the
   bottom.
And you'd flush that voice away.

NOTES FOR LIGHTING A FIRE

GERRY CAMBRIDGE

£8.00

2nd, paperback, edition available now from the HappenStance Press website. This second edition contains five new poems not in the first edition.

www.happenstancepress.com

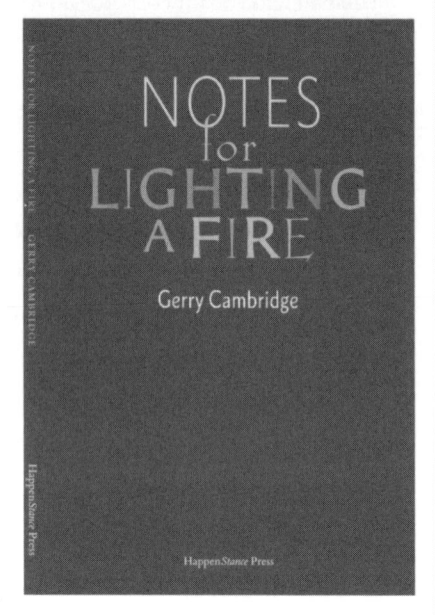

NOTES for LIGHTING A FIRE

Gerry Cambridge

HappenStance Press

FROM REVIEWS OF THE
HARDBACK EDITION

'[Cambridge's] poetry has something of Robert Frost's tone and seriousness, but rings with a deeply personal Scottish resonance all its own.'
—Rory Waterman,
The Times Literary Supplement

'...poetry of an extraordinary quality... as fresh as the coldest air of a winter's night.'
—Alison Brackenbury,
New Walk Magazine

'The language is simple, the effect beautiful, the craft-work sure. There is no affected elegance here, only a genuine elegance in the linguistic operation of almost every line.'
—John Foy, *Contemporary Poetry Review*

LUKE CARMAN
A Portrait of the Artist in Residence

Fond memories first: the grey-skinned trees and the hill-dimpled fields of the Kingswood campus crowded up to the windows of empty classrooms, the outside idyll bisected by the distant murmur of the Great Western Highway. Our group would meet once a fortnight in those eerily quiet and disorderly rooms between the bustle of tutorials where Marshall McLuhan quotations had dried onto the whiteboards and I will admit to rolling my eyes at the others when they buried their heads in notebooks or read deeply from their manuscripts. They were typical undergrads I suppose: a girl named Allison who was pretentiously in love with the 'bohemian' boy, Eddy; two tiny twins from the Mountains who synchronised their outfits and plaited their hair like characters from a children's cartoon; a shaggy bearded laddie from Kingswood who wore hipster glasses (this was in a time long before the term hipster came to mean almost anything to do with the white middle-class world); and a revolving host of wannabe poets and posers who so closely resembled one another that they have become unified by the clumsiness of retrospect.

To be sincere with you, I thought I knew more about every available world than all these comrades combined, on account of being beaten, repeatedly, by skater-skinhead-homeboys and meth-mangled houseos on the streets of Liverpool in my youth, and also because I'd trawled through the mania of all Henry Miller's classics in the Werrington library between semesters, alone on the empty hills of the campus while the others spent their free time playing pool at the uni bar, drunk, discussing sustainable ethics between the cracking clop of the balls and timid hollering at the bar staff about the patriarchy. All they knew about literature, I reckoned, was how to make cutting remarks on Hemingway's machismo. For example: one night, coaxed into the social world by one of the pixie-sized twins, who said, slinging her arm up toward my shoulder, 'Stop being so negative, it's such a clichéd attempt at seriousness through cynicism and it's just sad – y'know there's a lot going on that you can't even imagine, don't you? You won't learn anything stuck in your room like a hamster in a colon.' Her slight eyes leered at me through some sort of amphetamine high. In the bar, name forgotten, Eddy scoffed when I mentioned loving *The Old Man and the Sea* for its flagellant misery. I didn't mind him scoffing at my readings, but the next thing I knew his tobacco cleft breath slid into my nostrils; he leant toward me on his pool cue, like a gargoyle clinging to a doorframe, and he said, 'Hemingway's problem was that he was afraid he'd never be as much of a man as Gertrude Stein.' *What did I care about Hemingway?* I wondered looking at the grin Eddy bore me as he moved back toward the pool table; Papa was just another headless horseman as far as I was concerned, but to say something like that about the man – something Eddy'd no doubt stolen from a YouTube debate between Martin Amis and Terry Eagleton – shook me around like an eight-ball and the light in the room was almost as loud as the Hip Hop classics on the playlist (all black music was played ironically in Penrith back in those days). Next to a dancefloor the size of a coffin, the twins were sitting on stools and they nodded in solemn agreement about Ayn Rand having nothing to offer re the problems of the blooming 21st century – a subject Eddy had meandered into. The shaggy-faced hipster could confirm this perspective, having recently read an article online about Late Era Capitalism and Slavoj Žižek's theory of Divine violence which said pretty much the same thing.

It was possible I was just jealous, lacked charisma, but then again, I wasn't the only one who left early that night: Dani, the person I've held back from describing so far, as if it were some sort of secret, in fact was our leader – and as such, if for no other reason, I ought to have dedicated some time to her already. Earlier in the night, she took a dart from the board on the wall and told Eddy, who she was taller than by a head on account of his terrible posture and her thick Blundstone boots, 'The cult of the self is a shallow grave, and Rand was pushing on an open door, far as that goes – but I doubt anyone here has read a single word, outside of a title, or inside a cover, of one of her books – specially not you, Ed.' They all laughed with her, softly, supposing it was a joke, except Eddy, who rolled up his sleeves as he skulked to the bar and pawed at it, timidly, like a tiger who'd leapt and failed, and I could imagine him leaving later in the evening with the waifish Allison who sat beside the twins – she was smoking and staring out from under her fringe at the hunched figure of her paramour, and I could almost taste them going through their dorm room door together, crashing through it like lovers in a romantic comedy; their bodies wrapped together at the shoulders, his arms loose and sliding to her insignificant hips, the smell of his black, curling hair a rich cigarette stink.

Afterwards, with his ego avenged, they would lie in bed together, toes cold and a narrow, uneven slump of sheets and mattress keeping them close to waking, with the campus gum trees scratching on the window as they dreamed second-hand dreams of Hélène Cixous' poems that they'd ripped from the unit readers for subjects with names like *Writing Praxis in the Contemporary* and *Nomadic Modes of Visual Rhetoric*.

Dani and I left – coincidentally – together that night; she took her leave by the back and I went out front, unnoticed, our paths intersecting in the dark which had somehow consumed the sound of our footsteps. She started when we first saw one another in the shadows and said, 'Jesus you scared me,' with her eyes suspiciously slit.

'He scares me, too,' I told her, not sure if it was a joke and instantly ashamed of having said it.

The moon was in every window of the empty buildings on the campus, and the strange squat lanterns along the paths were filled with dying insect silhouettes. In an unspoken agreement – negotiated with careful oscillations in our pace – we walked to the end of the road together.

'I hate that twit,' I said to her, referring – I hoped it was clear – to Eddy. She didn't say a word, and now the sound of us walking and the armada of gum trees beyond the edge of the campus felt oppressive. I took a long look at Dani's pale profile in the dark but the night had arranged her curled blonde hair so as to obscure every clue from me, and I tell you that didn't seem fair, and the walk went on in silence until at last I said, 'I have to go to the train station.'

For a moment, I thought she was about to laugh, though I wasn't quite sure why she might find a comment like that amusing.

'Good luck,' she said without looking, and turned, without so much as a farewell wave, down a path through the park on way to the dorms and I let out a sigh, suddenly aware of a painful feeling, as though my shoulders had carried an enormous weight.

The next week we met as normal. There was a game we played as a collective in those chair-scattered rooms with the bald light flickering above us and the air-conditioner blowing like the burner of a hot-air balloon from the ribbed vent in the corner. It was Dani's Game – a house-rules adaptation of Exquisite Corpse in which you were asked to 'Write a sentence, fold the paper, pass it on' until Dani decided it was time to read. I didn't think it was much of an exercise. Dani – being a woman stepped directly from a Jane Austen fan club – didn't think much of my sentences, so I thought. She crossed her legs with a careful pull at an ankle-length skirt and the toffee-thick curls shook and her bosom was strapped tight to her chest beneath a lime green top. In the case of Dani, it feels right to use the word 'bosom', since there seemed to me something out of step with time and language about her, either too late or too early in existence for my thoughts and words to brush against without dislocating, becoming archaic. She unfurled the group's resulting narrative and read it aloud – it was always her job to read things aloud – and the outcome, as always, was an elegant nonsense of prose all the way to the last syllable, and I scoffed silently as her eyebrows arched and her lips squeezed loose the final full stop. I detested how repetitive each exercise came to be, how gentle and domestic – and how co-operative everyone tried to be – because I was dumb and young enough to believe there was something worthwhile about Miller's descriptions of wing-led erections and obsessing with the fields outside filled with ghosts on the run from history – which was the sum total of Australian literature in my cynical readings of Henry Lawson and Christos Tsiolkas.

Indeed, in the mode of cynic, I made much sport of Dani with my girlfriend at the time, a Greek Anglo girl with long black hair and eyes dark and evil enough to make me want to hold to her in the night – the kind of girl I liked in those delirious days.

Outside in the car park after our group meetings my girlfriend would have her Commodore running for me, the 'done-up' exhaust shuddering like a pawing lion on the crest of the hilly campus, and as we'd ricochet onto the highway she would say, 'Tell me, Pendragon, what happened in your stupid group this time.' I'd tell her whatever absurdity Dani had ended on, for instance, according to her, Nabokov had told his students that the most essential requirement for becoming a great reader was a sense of their own spinal column. My girlfriend, whom I don't wish to name and who, for some reason, gave to me the title of British kings, would expose her crooked teeth as she grinned at these accounts, smiling to herself while I watched the university receding in the passenger's wing mirror, my thoughts straying for a moment to Dani's dangling blonde curls and her pale blue sternness, like a shallow pond on a spring afternoon. My hand wound its way into my girlfriend's hair and onto the pale skin at the nape of her neck, while the uni was swallowed by accelerating distance.

But I did not tell my girlfriend about the time Dani came to my sentence when the afternoon light was low, and, by God, in front of the whole group, hesitated. It was the final meeting of that feeble cohort, and the exchange between Dani and I was something not to be shared. It all went as clockwork, up until she unfurled the corpse as always, standing at the front of the class with the rest of us arranged in chairs like her personal scholars, hand-picked for the honour of following every elegant moment of her precise pronunciation. But this time, how I tripped her up good! In a moment of electrified rebellion

I had invented, though it is hard to explain it now, a sentence I was sure would be a spanner in her proverbial works. And I was right! For the briefest of moments I had her frozen as the ice-man's tomb! It may seem absurd, but I tell you Dani's sudden halt in narration was a tremendous victory for an undergrad like me, and as it occurred my whole body tensed to the point of sweating. It was, as I am saying, something orgasmic – though that doesn't do it justice at all. It's hard to explain, but I'm sure you have met people like Dani – people who never seem likely to strike something unexpected in their lives, and you can see in their calm eyes that they will forever sail across the surface of life's injustices, seeing the universe divided, however arbitrarily, into the ocean and the sky as they pass over it with an even keel cutting through that which is beneath them . . . Anyway, that's how it was with Dani, and when she halted, I felt like a great fish who had learned to crawl, just for a moment, from her sea into her sky. The class was quiet and the slightest wriggle of panic made itself known on every blank face in the room. Eddy alone was willing to break the quiet – he crossed his arms over an Elmo-buttoned hoodie and furrowed his brow and said, 'What's wrong Dani?' Her cocoa-tanned lips mouthed the syllables I'd written and I knew she was struck by something sickly, something devilish. I might as well tell you the truth, although it doesn't make for good reading. I'd written: 'Satan punched the horse in the head.' The twins laughed when she said it aloud, confused, it seemed to me, and then Dani read it again to herself. The group – I don't know how to explain this – suddenly became a mass of lonely bodies (except perhaps the twins) and everyone saw for a moment that they were deceiving themselves if they had ever thought, even for a moment, that the world they could see and hear and taste was there to be shared with anyone else. Perhaps I am overdoing it, but I believe it was a good lesson for a room full of writers. In any case, it is easier to say that the contagion of shame flared through the room like fire, and the way the sun was setting made it seem as though the classroom was beginning to blush.

Dani's brown eyebrows, which were slowly sinking, started to twitch, and the others shifted in their seats. She thought it over. The twins looked at one another, and the bearded boy in his hipster spectacles glanced over thin rims at me with a quizzical affectation, unsure which way the winds would blow.

'What does it mean?' Dani asked, her hand still clutching the accordion manuscript our collective had created.

'I don't know,' I replied.

She looked around and her eyes were filled with a heaviness that might have been annoyance.

Danielle cancelled the group. She shut it down for all time. The others filed out. Eddy with his arm around Allison, the twins and the hipster with their heads low shuffled off toward the uni bar to work out where the world had gone wrong. By another unspoken agreement, Dani and I stayed until it was just the two of us left: she sat on a desk, arms folded over the Exquisite Corpse, crushing and cradling it all at once as I slowly rose from my seat.

'Why'd you end the group like that?' I asked her. 'Can't you put up with one ugly sentence?' I tried to keep eye contact, but her eyes were too blue and the room seemed to get heavy with the light leaving the sky and weighing on us alone, so that our reflections appeared on the windows like parallel witnesses to our exchange.

'Look at where and who you are,' she said as I picked up my bag of *Sexus*, *Plexus* and *Nexus*, nervous she might recognise their shape and see through the whole affair. 'You're not a new thing, you're a fossil of the old world – you and every man-child like you, and, for your own sake, change – before we all get bored to death.'

Dani and I never saw one another again as undergrads. Except in my dreams – where, for no reason, for nothing to do with what happened in the anaemia of that memory, Dani's pale phantom would walk the streets of Liverpool, past the slowly rising apartment blocks and the burning council chambers and the cemetery gates, and up the small mountain toward my house with its high view of the surrounding suburbs. I'd roll in the damp sheets and toss my head, and she'd follow me into Westfield parking lots and Chinese restaurant alleyways (sometimes in nothing but a green raincoat), her curls tinged silver in the moonlight and the blue of her eyes like the curved edge of a spoon held up to the stars. She would sprawl at the head of my bed some nights, and pace the halls of libraries in ruby-coloured shoes. I thought, in waking life, of contacting Dani. Her name occasionally appeared in the Australasian Literary Society mailing lists, or on academic conference tables. In the café strips of Newtown's High street where the sun was always setting and spilt-red twilight cascaded upon the rooftops, I thought once or twice I'd caught sight of her curls, disguised by a new style or updated to suit the season. It made no sense, and I could not change with the times.

All this would have come to no more than a wishful pornography (and if you ask me, that's all there is on Earth to say about creative writing groups and the people caught in them, waiting patiently for the end of their artfulness, like lice-preening birds, perched a-twitter around a shit-stuck windowsill) but for an email that came my way a few weeks ago.

The email was nondescript, full of formalities. It asked me, on behalf of the University of Wollongong, to come and be an artist in residence for their writing programme. This was not surprising. After all, my collection, *A Dozen Doorbells on the House of Time*, had won the Prime Minister's Award for New Writing. Since that win, the invitations had come thick and fast, and being overwhelmed I stayed in my room and deleted them so as to convince myself that they had never occurred. The nondescript email from the Wollongong University would have been no different, but the name at the bottom gave me occasion to halt the cursor above the little digital garbage can. It was signed, sincerely, by Dani – now, apparently, a senior lecturer in English. I closed the trap of my laptop and shivered so hard that the knots in my spine cracked. I rose from my bed-ridden slump with a thrill of dread and ecstasy.

'We can offer accommodation, at the campus lodge, should you require it.' A strange sentence that stood out as somehow enigmatic amidst the propriety of the rest of the email. Or was I reading wrongly, confused by my own suppressions and dreams? Even now, I am not sure if there is something meaningful about that sentence, but nevertheless, it thrilled me to find it in my inbox. Immediately, my mind filled with fantasies of seeing Dani again – this time, both of us adults; accomplished, seasoned and wise.

As it turned out, I was the only man, woman, child at the lodge during my stay on the oddly isolated island of Wollongong University. A security guard in dark blue uniform towered over me at the entrance of the campus and made me repeat my name three times before going upstairs into the huge concrete expanse of the administrative office to find the keys for my accommodation. When she returned she sternly handed me a card and pointed to a number underlined on it. 'That's the number to call if you need any help,' she said, almost threateningly. She was vague, too, on directions, and I circled the campus three or four times trying to turn down the right road toward the lodge.

The keys fed me to room number six. The key-ring included a large metallic disc, perhaps to prevent it being treated carelessly, engraved with a dog's head that also resembled a dove. On entering the apartment I threw down my bags and stripped off all clothes, and ran naked and flapping up to the bathroom mirror as if to catch it by surprise; but what would you know! It surprised me! With the weak light of the late afternoon behind me, I was alarmed by the glow of my own muscularity, thought it, for a moment, a stranger, and in a panic, hurled a flurry of punches at the reflective figure who, after the initial shock subsided, became, in mind's eye, a local critic named Stephen Triste who had treated me badly. I hated him and his stupid sentiments. Often we would fight in my head. Always I won. In Triste's Twitter picture he looks solid of jaw and thoughtful; hand curled around chin to demonstrate the weight of his mind at work. I wasn't sure how the fighting would go when this image was the extent of my acquaintance with him. Later, at some sad affair at the writers centre in Rozelle, I saw that his profile picture was one of those magic moments in his life when he had looked good. In motion, as he descended a long staircase in that old colonial relic, his jaw was a wispy thing and his shaved head balanced like the bulb of an un-burned match propped atop a fleshless framework of pencil-thin elbows, knees and neck. After that vision of him – plodding down the old staircase with two complimentary cupcakes in his hand and a lanyard around his neck, like a puppet in a noose – he fought poorly in my fantasies, his wild swings bouncing off my head, and I would go so far as to say the fantasies weren't fun any more. Triste wrote in his review of *A Dozen Doorbells* that I risked becoming a mouthpiece and losing all artfulness. What a thing to write! Only a man as thin and frail as him could write such drivel! Immediately after reading the review I looked up his own writing on the internet and consoled myself that he was a talentless hack inflamed by envy at my success.

When night came upon the lodge, I lay on the made bed, having written my lecture for Dani's students, and I rolled into a dream of chasing Triste through the science quad at my old high school, with the September sun blinking at me through the crow-crowded ghost gums. In the dream I was long-haired again, a young man, soft with baby fat, and I grinned as we ran through the breezeway past the toilet blocks, and Triste, a miniature version of himself, had Sophocles or something stoic tucked tightly to his chest. He was beginning to wheeze with asthma and terror, and he hoped, I knew, that the mysterious dignity of ancient times would bleed from the book into his cowardly heart, or at least transport some dimension of his essence into the long gone past, which, since it is only written down in books, seems so much less shameful than the living nightmare of a boys school in Liverpool with bright blue spikes and barbed wire wrung around its head like a crown of steely thorns. There was no intent in my heart to catch him, only to herd him out onto the sports field until we both collapsed into the buffalo grass with pure blue above us – me laughing tears of happiness, him crying into the grubby earth and beating his bird-boned fists into its hardness. That's all, to lay there for a while, history rewritten.

When I awoke from that dream, I didn't know whether it was still the first night at the lodge, or the second day. The curtains were drawn and the clock was unplugged. My phone was dead and I could not find the charger. The lecture notes lay on the table beside the bed. They were, I realised with dawning terror, an indulgent litany of jokes in bad taste. I promised myself I wouldn't swear during the lecture on this occasion, since it always shamed both myself and the students, and of course Dani, too, would frown on it, but I knew somehow that I would do it anyway.

What a strange thing. I dressed and gathered my notes and went down the stairs with my feet echoing off stucco. It made me turn back a few times to see no one following behind, and I felt, stupidly, great pity for the maid who must go up to my room on those stairs soon only to see that the lone guest did not wish to be disturbed.

On my way out I hesitated at the double doors of the lodge's conference room. It was on the ground floor, right by the entrance, and it was locked, but my room key worked it open. It would shame me greatly to tell you why I opened the doors, but I might as well be honest – I secretly hoped to see Dani waiting for me inside. She was not, of course. Inside there was a long table with little speakers in its centre; ten chairs, all out of fashion by several decades but well maintained or underused – some scratches along the wooden surfaces the only sign of life – and an old stereo behind glass in the corner. The lake outside the room, which I'd spent some time staring into on first arrival, was too dark to make out, but its watery presence seemed to press up against the lodgings in the darkness as if it might make a move into the dreams of guests – dreams in which the whole squat brick building would perhaps slump sideways toward the lake and sink cartoon-like beneath the mud.

I sat at the head of the table, finding by the wall something to plug my phone into, and felt like a chieftain's body at a conference of ghosts before I noticed a tattered dart board displayed on the hip-high cupboards. I plucked out a single dart and sat back down at the head of the table to toss it across the wide empty room – the green fins whirled and the dart's needle sunk uncannily into the bullseye. What a shot! It truly was one in a million from where I was sitting, and I leapt up and punched the air in triumph before I could restrain myself. I stole a glance at the glass doors as if expecting God to be standing there shaking his head at this loss of control, but it was too dark outside to see anything for certain. Somebody, not the Lord, obviously, might have been watching me from the gloom: a stray senior lecturer maybe, wandering the campus and spying through the curtains of the lodge like a poet in search of her desires. Nevertheless, it didn't matter – no one was around. I sat back at the table, feeling oddly uncomfortable about the way my legs were angled. Who had sat here before? I wondered, bouncing a little on the burgundy cushion as though there might be something in its propulsion that my arse might divine in way of an answer. What a strange thing to do, I decided, and besides: was that the best question I could come up with? I had to ask myself: Is that the sort of query Maurice Blanchot would ponder were he caught alone at night in a Parisian tavern? His name made its way into the mix of my thoughts because one of his books was in the lodge, slumped to the side of the library shelf, apparently recently read. Taking the book's displacement as a hint of its quality, I had read the first pages – something about a stranger who wanders into the city and is held, indefinitely, in detention for his own happiness and the sake of the people. The story was ruined by the local atmosphere of the country, where such questions came too shamefully close to the bone. Instead of enjoying the spare prose, I made creative writing critiques in the margins: 'more detail needed – we don't get much description of the protagonist's physicality, and there is little to no specificity regarding the setting – without these things it is hard to connect with the story'. It gave me great pleasure to correct a famous Frenchman.

Eventually, my phone charged and the sun rose and, just as I started to doze in my chair, it seemed suddenly to be time to go and give the lecture. I wandered along a duck-dotted path that wound its way into the campus amidst the lively chatter of students swarming the university in the cool morning air, their hands in pockets and chins tucked into scarves. I followed the directions Dani had sent me to a large lecture room. A fat man with thinning hair on his round head was standing behind the lectern, in front of a huge wall onto which a computer desktop image of an Appalachian mountain was projected. He greeted me with a meaty handshake. His name was Damien, and he informed me, with his slight eyes squeezed in fierce welcome that he'd read and loved *A Dozen Doorbells*.

'Where's Dani?' I asked.

Damien frowned and his jowls dropped down from his jaw. 'Oh! Professor Herrick is on a residency in Paris! I apologise if that wasn't clear – but to be honest, I was the one who asked her to invite you. I think *A Dozen Doorbells on the House of Time* is a masterpiece – a total inversion of Australian voice! It is not, as it happens, completely unlike some of my own work! I'm very pleased to have you here . . . Anyway, I'll tell you all my thoughts afterwards; here come the students – they've all read your book too you know!'

Damien eased into his front-row seat and winked at me, smiling openly while the room filled with young people and their mumbled, morning chatter. The persistent interjection of the lecture-room door slamming shut gave the students' muttered exchanges a savage punctuation. The talk was titled *Writing the Sub-City*, and I intended to show them an extract from Antigone Kefala's journals in order to demonstrate to Dani that I had moved away from Henry Miller. I needed her to know that I was no longer obsessed with erections made of lead and the ghosts that are lost on university campuses.

The students shrugged through the hour and shifted in their seats. To make matters worse, I had left my copy of Kefala's journals back in the lodge, and I said so to them aloud – like this: 'I'd like to draw your attention to . . . something I've left back at the apartment!' I thought it would make at least some of them snicker to say it that way, but I heard nothing except my finger smacking the microphone stand when I turned back to the slideshow on the lectern computer.

In her journals, I explained to the furrowed brows on the bright white faces, Kefala says that when she first came out of Europe she and her friends suffered from the lack of historical weight in the air and water, along the streets of the city and in the cemeteries with their milky white accoutrements through which strong winds were always blowing and the pool-blue sky seemed so garish and indifferent to elemental human life. Growing older, I told them, as Kefala grows too, I begin to see how foolish a thing that is to say, how archaic a vision she was sketching. Then again, I admitted, in this new century, that I barely recognise, with its inverted myths of slouch-hatted soldiers, their ghostly images projected onto the Harbour Bridge at night, or slung in laser-light upon the sepulchral curves of the Opera House – with the lighthorsemen eternally staked into the earth between the crossed legs of the colossal motorways paved over the arse of the western suburbs – it would be hard to argue with the high tone Kefala takes, and all her perceptions of emptiness. Beside Damien, whose jowl flexed and shook its way through the talk, more attentive to my voice than its owner, I thought, who held his hand up to tap at the bum of his chin on occasion, his tight eyes darting over everything in the room, was an empty seat. If Dani was not in Paris, I supposed, as I read from my notes, she would be sitting in that seat. If she were here, her long curls, I realised, would be the only golden element in the horrid hermeneutics of the lecture room.

'If you lose the flow of your story, your setting, your characters, for even a moment – it's all gone and you've fucked it.' I said. They shifted, listless in their seats, with a thousand pantomimes of indifference all upon me at once. Death was in their youthful gaze.

Later, back in the conference room with my board of the dead, I tossed the second dart. Unbelievable! I said with wide eyes. Another bullseye! This time it was the one with the blue fin, like a swordfish, I thought. It was stuck into the red centre of the board perfectly alongside the earlier miracle – the two darts suddenly appearing like lovers. No celebration this time: just a disembodied smile. In the dark windows of the room I saw the expression's glow reflected back at me. It was only a faint reflection on the surface of the glass, and now only a memory, but what a lonely smile it was.

GABRIELLE WITTKOP
from *Each Day Is a Tree that Falls*

Chaque jour est un arbre qui tombe by Gabrielle Wittkop (Gallimard/Verticales, 2006); translated from the French by Louise Rogers Lalaurie

Appropriately for a title with the unmistakeable ring of a tolling bell, Each Day Is a Tree that Falls was published posthumously after being found among Gabrielle Wittkop's papers by her old friend and literary executor Nikola Delescluse. Like the rest of her extraordinary oeuvre, Wittkop's last book is a celebration of death and life, Eros and Thanatos, beauty and ugliness, friendship and cruelty, frailty, transgression, and the freedom of the spirit.

Gabrielle Wittkop (née Menardeau) was born in Nantes, in 1920. Self-educated in her father's extensive, liberal library, she read 'd'Alembert, Holbach, Diderot, Sade at a very young age. I was a child of the Enlightenment.' She died by her own hand in Frankfurt, in 2002, after being diagnosed with lung cancer. In a letter to her editor Bernard Wallet, she declared her intention 'to die as I have lived, a free man.' It was a characteristically unorthodox end to a colourful life that saw her interned as a collaborator in Paris in 1945, for hiding and then marrying Justus Wittkop, a homosexual German deserter twenty years her senior. (Wittkop herself was bisexual, and the two enjoyed 'a marriage of friendship and affection' in Germany until Justus's suicide, aged 87, when he was diagnosed with Parkinson's disease.) Wittkop wrote for the culture pages of the Frankfurter Allgemeiner Zeitung *and worked for the pharmaceutical firm Hoffman-Laroche, travelling widely in Europe and throughout Asia. Her first book was a biography of the German Romantic E. T. A. Hoffman, followed eight years later by a novel,* The Necrophiliac, *published when she was 52. Almost forty years later, this was also the first of her works to appear in English, translated by*

Don Pabst (ECW Press, 2011). Marking perhaps the farthest outpost of Wittkop's distinctive territory, the book offers nothing less than a detailed meditation on the sensual delights of dead flesh, 'so soft, so cold, so deliciously tight'. Guardian critic Nicholas Lezard hailed it as 'a masterpiece' but felt compelled to 'slowly put the book back in my pocket' when reading it on the London Underground. Two more works have since been brought into English by Wakefield Press: Exemplary Departures *(translated by Annette David) and* Murder Most Serene *(in my translation)* are nearer to the centre ground, but they contain much that is calculated to shock and stir, nonetheless. The first chronicles the 'departures' of figures including Edgar Allen Poe, Thai silk dealer Jim Thompson, and Claude and Hippolyte (aristocratic hermaphrodite twins in 18th-century France), while in Murder Most Serene, *mysterious poisonings cause Venetian ladies to 'burst like wineskins' in a city that is the epitome of beauty and rottenness.*

For readers new to her work, both are fine showcases for Wittkop's central preoccupations – death and the macabre, corruption and transgression, with more than a hint of Grand Guignol. Each Day is a Tree that Falls *is no exception*. Wittkop's childhood memories, travels and enthusiasms are distilled in a fictionalised biography of the imagination. In places, the writing is radiant with her passion for art, her unerring sense of beauty and melancholy; in others, it is 'as duteous to the [fascinations] of its mistress as badness could desire' (Edgar's phrase in King Lear *was never more apt)*. Wittkop was a proud exponent of the French extrême littéraire, unstinting in her depiction of the darkest in human nature, serving up choice set-pieces of (superficially) amoral detachment in the best tradition of the genre. (And yes, as a fellow delegate once observed to me at a Paris conference on the subject, 'something terrible always happens to a nun'.) Wittkop is unflinching, then, but not, I think, pitiless. Her description of the sufferings of an Indian child god springs from a profoundly humane empathy. Never one to 'not go there', her determination to observe and document, with an objective realism akin to photo-reportage, is an act of empathy in itself. Wittkop was revolted by poverty ('it stinks,' she once said, in an interview), but she is *revolted by what poverty makes people endure, too. In this dysfunctional nativity scene, the narrator Hippolyte's contempt for the child's profiteering family is plain to see.*

In Venice, the text strolls like an intrigued tourist into more dangerous territory, as far beyond the pale as anything in Wittkop's writing, and as darkly humorous, too. We may even smile in spite of ourselves, and this sets our moral compass spinning uncomfortably, as she so clearly intended.

Each Day Is a Tree that Falls is full of Wittkop's characteristic wit and transgressive zeal, but there's a more wistful, elegiac quality, too. The dizzying plunges into Hippolyte's subconscious, and the vivid tapestry of characters and settings, from childhood Nantes to Rome, Venice, India and Indonesia, are held in an astonishing web of visual and formal echoes that operates on a quite different, subliminal level (almost as a kind of safety net). Boarding a plane at sunset, Hippolyte finds that: 'As always, the flight puts her in a trance, opening and structuring her thoughts like the rose-window patterns of a mandala.' That spirit of fearless, mindful receptiveness is our key to this book, to its myriad imaginative connections, and its unexpected beauties.

— L.R.L.

India

Pages torn from the secret narrative of a journey through India. Recapitulative notes inseparable from the figure of the Canadian sales representative, if only for his role as a simple informer. Hippolyte first met the little Canadian salesman in the post office on the M.I. Road, after spotting him several times at the cashier's window at the bank, white-scarved, red and inflamed like some carefully bandaged whitlow. He sees a great many things on his wanderings, peddling thalidomide fraudulently saved from destruction in Europe, and prescribed by him against toothache.

'The poor always have toothache,' says the little Canadian trader, quietly. 'About the hermaphrodite I mentioned, you can see it at Brahma Puri, behind the tea shop, opposite the little temple of Shiva. Look around, ask around . . .'

An old, half-naked man shows her the way, amid rose-coloured rocks, the barred shade of colonnades that dazzle the eye, belvederes topped with Moghul helmets. He guides her between real surfaces and imagined spaces, hybrid prospects of geometry and equations, and the lively gait of the lines of a poem, a perpetual outburst of circles and spirals twirling like new cotton flowers, chromosome structures or the movement of ocean currents. Yet everything seems insubstantial, ethereal, a translucent shell through which one might pass with ease. Already, winter is retreating; the first flies alight on the lips. The languid odour of pestilence and excrement rises with the miasma from Ramgarh Lake, its polished black mud reflecting the kiosks.

To the mournful song of a dove on a wall, Hippolyte steps inside a hut of planks and corrugated iron, a stable of sorts, decorated with paper flowers, pious images and streamers. An indecipherable extended family surrounds a child of about eight, lying on a foul mattress, in a slanting shaft of sunlight. The child is naked apart from a tangled mass of necklaces, ribbons, amulets, a great ornamental jabot falling across its chest. Its skin is ashen with white patches of vitiligo, the body both frail and bloated, the hair matted and thin. The forehead is enormous above eyes daubed in black kohl. The only sounds are the dove, far off now, the child's almost uninterrupted coughing, and the murmur of prayer. Hippolyte pays her contribution and lights an incense stick standing in a bottle. An old woman with metallic blue skin places a mala garland around her neck. Hippolyte approaches the child who, on its mattress, seems not to see her, or anything else. Its mouth, cheek and ornaments are coated in saliva. Its penis – a counterfeit, apparently mummified worm above a slit that may well have been opened with a knife, sticking out barely any further than the large, shapeless belly button – lies as if waiting, longing, for the great abdomen to swallow it up. Prone to a tic that causes it to wink continually, the child brings forth another image, a bright pebble in the muddied waters of memory. Hippolyte remembers how, as a little girl, she was taken by her mother to visit one of her aunts, committed to the Perpetual Adoration of the Blessed Sacrament. She retained the curious impression of an utterly mute woman in a white court mantle marked with red, her blond-Chinese face agitated by an incessant tic. In the persistent, rhythmic winking, like a recurrent drip of water, Hippolyte had sensed some hint of vice, though she could not, then, discern its nature: a libidinous, certainly secret appeal, like that encountered later in life when, to get a better look, she would adjust her glasses in the gloom of some sleazy bar.

An angry-faced man, a man the colour of a louse, gives her to understand that the child is an incarnation of the hermaphrodite god Shiva Ardhanarisvara. She has seen him before. A few months earlier, carved in stone at Elephanta, crowned with an infinite, burgeoning tiara of oceanic pullulations, spiralling galaxies, she beheld the lord of the ages, Shiva Ardhanarisvara, with his pendulous breasts, his round hips swelling beneath the draperies, his masculine face framed by curls and carbuncles, the pectorals fat and fleshy but square, the sharply tapering flank, the bare, robust leg and, hidden under bracelets, one arm resting on the bull Nandi while the other, veiled, swathed in linen and modesty, held a rose.

Obsequious, eager to please, the extended family asks if Madam can see well enough, and offers – for an additional contribution – to have the child urinate in her presence: a curiosity. The child barely raises itself, stirring up a stench of carrion. The old woman with the metallic skin supports the child under the armpits while another holds a rusty can between the deity's thighs, an empty tin of green beans into which the child releases its water, shuddering, before falling back onto the mattress, taking with it a last thin trail of urine; of corrupted blood, too. Eyes closed, it looks suddenly dead. Outside, the dove's cooing halts abruptly, hollowing a void. The man with the louse-coloured skin takes hold of the can and steps outside, chanting incantations. The urine would be drunk, undoubtedly. The child lifts its eyelids, gazing straight through Hippolyte, indifferent – but with malice, hatred or reproach, perhaps, behind the eye's black, glassy pane. The gods are irascible. She must say nothing, write nothing. The child closes its eyes. Mystery, the great raven, folds its wings. Hippolyte steps out into the light of the setting sun that daubs the hilltops, the ramshackle kiosks, shells. In her dreams she inhabits the shell of the nautilus, swimming the timeless, Cambrian seas, born aloft on effervescent clouds, solitary, insensate, traversing incalculable distances, dark nights, processions of phosphorescent jellyfish. She steps outside and walks away, prayers and lamentations at her back, through the beggars, the dusty fowl and spittle.

*

Here, then, the ancient gnostic symbol, the model of all perfection, the occult paragon of ages past, painted in gold and cerumen on the secret pages of the Nuremberg chronicle, a shield in one hand, in the other, the universal egg. Here at last, then, the hermaphrodite I had thought to be my brother, my reflected image, whom I longed to meet one day, like Goethe crossing his double on a bridge. But the mirror plays tricks, it seems. At least it does so here.

*

I have seen another hermaphrodite, though he too may have been a pretender to the title. A creature in a yellow wig, outside a butcher's shop on the corner of Rue de la Montaigne-Sainte-Geneviève: a one-legged tout standing firmly on his stump, dressed in an age-old crêpe haute-couture gown, the mouth daubed as if with betel juice, eyes rimmed charcoal-black, decked all over in rabbit-skin and jade, a denizen of the underworld, an ephebe of the gutter, clattering his wooden leg on the greasy, rounded cobbles. The creature had come, it was said, from a brothel in Le Havre for mariners who have seen it all. Sometimes I saw putty-coloured trench coats, miserable houndstooth or worn-out Prince-of-Wales checks walking with him towards the glaring signs of a sordid hotel. The stench of fries filled the air. Shouting was heard, and radios. And close by, yet far away, the sigh of the Seine.

*

Blinking behind dark glasses, her gaze follows the flight of a vulture, that richly, profoundly resonant bird. Hippolyte loves the distant bird, its feathers fringing the celestial blue; loves it like chastity, a thing out of reach. In the same way, she had loved a paper kite, a great golden dragon, slightly torn, that the wind had gently removed from her grasp, one day in childhood: suddenly the string was no longer between her fingers and there it was, up high, suspended in the pale purple sky where no bird flew, the pale purple sea where no boat passed, not even trying to escape, but intangible, irrevocably gone, gone forever yet present still, motionless and yellow and superb. Running on the pebbles, crying far below, Hippolyte had loved the kite for being lost, loved it like a dead friend.

*

Motionless and yellow and superb, the long saffron chrysalis encountered on the M.I. Road, the dead man, the unknown man borne like a dead king, a golden tree of death carried to the pyres, where the vultures gather. Like the fallen trees, the floating logs of Atjeh, before, in Sumatra, I remember . . . The precious wood moved down the great river. The great silver sterculias beloved of birds of prey, the dragon trees, and the rosewood still bloodied with red, floating downstream to the estuaries, where they formed continents, mobile archipelagos, rafts pushed like folds of drapery by men silhouetted in black, tracing lines along the Alas River, long plumes of water, reaching to the horizon barred abruptly by the crowns of their brethren, moving with the current, recumbent like dead kings, recumbent like the dead man dressed in gold whose cortège I did not follow. I remember. Unless I forget, for there is, too, the vast charnel house of my dead grey cells, my photographic cells, of all that I have eliminated, casting off my encumbrances, though painful memories are not necessarily cumbersome memories. But always memory brings anxiety, the fear of losing myself in losing the things I want to keep, even if I could swallow myself down, a cave diver in the chasm of my own throat, descending eye and soul into the crinkled, undulating, nerve-patterned flesh of the oesophagus, to the darkest, deepest pit of my own insides.

*

Another morsel for this feast of memories . . . My childhood was morose but remarkable nonetheless, and rich in surprises, for I have always had the gift of seeing what people strove to hide. Which, in my childhood, was almost everything. Another half-folded paper, slightly ajar like this door, open the merest crack, just wide enough for my eye. A death, at once sordid and rarefied, perhaps. A death infinitely more outrageous than death itself. In the 1920s, whispered appeals are heard, stifled exclamations. From far off, I hear them; from far off, I come, down endless corridors. And so I hear: lamentations uttered *sotto voce*. A myopic child, I see it all. I half understand, but well enough, in the narrow space left ajar, the half-closed toilet door. For it becomes quite suddenly, quite brutally apparent that one of my uncles – the president of the Chamber of Commerce in a fine port city – has taken illicit pleasure in this private place and that such things may very well be a cause of death. I came upon the scene just as his sons were extricating him, the elder of the two supporting him by the seat while the younger, bearing the flaccid weight of the chest, which would keep tipping forward, found the dead father's face pressed close to his own, frozen in an expression of imbecilic beatitude, looming like a reflection in the back of a spoon. (The man thus deceased was Aunt Alice's father-in-law, grandfather to Huguette, one of us, one of the Atreides.) I was there, present in a gaping double door, in the interstices of memory, present and invisible – unless the scene's horrified players saw me unconsciously, unawares – though I had not perfectly understood, though I was but eight years old. Essentially, I knew nothing of the uncle but his name, and that he liked to compare himself to Talleyrand, because he walked with a limp. It was from him that I heard the name Talleyrand for the first time.

Venice

At that time of day when the water turns to light – pale, shimmering violet stained with a rainbow of oil – Hippolyte steps into Harry's Bar and is delighted to find Max, her childhood friend, the boy judged too light and frivolous by Huguette's (yes, Huguette's) parents, though he had never thought of marrying her. Thin as a sprig on a restaurant table, his shoulders lopsided, Max invariably has some curiosity to hand, retrieved from his memory or the bottom of a glass. Living on monies sent by a sister to whom he ceded the paternal sawmill, he taps at his wood-pile like a death watch beetle, a few grams of pulp for his whisky, a little sapwood for the cats' meat, a log for the rent, another for the housekeeper. He has devoured an entire warehouse already, keeping back one or two splendid cedars for dessert (the logs were destined for pencil manufacturers), and silk-smooth quipos set aside for the masts of yachts. Max lives as he always wanted to live, and hence as he deserves.

'This city in which we find ourselves is beautiful not only in shades of grey, but when the summer sun defines the deep lines of her face. I go everywhere, into courtyards and passages, into staircases, and garrets hot as ovens under the rooftiles. One day, I pushed on the door of a completely bare attic, deserted, coated in a soft felt of dust. I wrote on the door with a stick of rouge: *Love lessons here*.'

'This city . . .' says Max. 'As for the tourist froth, I consider it null and void, something it would be unseemly to talk about, a residual substance.'

'At night, beneath my windows, the water in the canal is black as ink. And in summer, every night at 10p.m., an absurd flotilla of gondolas passes by on this Styx. No, this is not melancholy Acheron, with the body of Sarpedon gliding downstream. No willows or reeds here, nothing but the lugubrious slop of black water, gondolas crammed with people who are perfect strangers, carried along listening to some fat matron singing with the accordion. Laughing, delighted, their faces pale as plaster in the operatic twilight, Japanese families and old American ladies meander along the Styx. Even when they return to their hotel, these people are dead. Dead without knowing it. And when all falls quiet, I see nothing from my window but a great windowless façade, the black water, and a municipal street lamp.

'You know very well that one can only settle in Venice as one might marry a dying woman. Venice is pink with all the blood it spits. Once, I made love to a woman who was as if dead, who played dead. Yes, here, in Venice. Two months ago. The housekeeper has the laundry done by nuns in a convent, S. M. d. G., and every Thursday afternoon two nuns bring the laundry back. They always come in twos. Well, I have no idea what might have happened to disrupt the conventual order, but one day I was surprised to see a washer-nun arriving in the singular. And it was a Wednesday. Wednesday is Teresa's free day and she had indeed left to see her family in Oriago. I was alone. It was very hot. Somewhat intimidated, the novice-ette claimed she didn't want to stay when I offered refreshment. I insisted. She accepted. The nun amused me. She was very young, with slightly reddened hands but a fine classical face and a hint of a slender waist beneath her habit. I served her several glasses of a mix of orange juice, champagne and gin which she swallowed like water. I poured and poured again. When you start, you just can't stop. Have you ever seen a nun completely drunk? Ah, very strange indeed. Their thoughts run instantly to sex. Like iron filings to a magnet. The nun kept repeating – though more and more languidly – that she didn't want to be late. At the same time, she allowed herself to be undressed, laughing up her sleeve and helping me to some extent, because it was a difficult undertaking. She had absolutely extraordinary underwear, archaic undergarments doubtless prescribed by the foundress of her order two or three hundred years ago, broad skirts of grey flannelette, a thick corset made of ticking, stockings held by suspenders and nothing resembling panties of any kind. Most strange, indeed. At first, I thought the nun wasn't on her maiden run, but I was wrong, she was a virgin. She went into a total faint during the act of love, and she wasn't faking. It wasn't a straightforward faint, more a kind of psychosomatic coma, involuntary and devoutly wished all at the same time, like the phenomenon of hysteria, and she was out for four hours. For four hours, I held this moribund woman in my arms, like a doll, breathing but not living. In the hope of bringing her round, I made love to her in every possible way. Yes, I did everything I could. For four hours. Finally, because I had had quite a bit to drink myself, I sat her on the bidet and I remember pissing down her spine – because I was annoyed by now – while holding her bust to stop her falling forwards. Imagine the scene. The good sister, stark naked, out cold for hours, filthy, slimy, flopping and swaying like a sack of potatoes on the bidet and me pissing down her back. I can't remember what effect it had on her. I was too drunk to care. I think I slept. I woke up late at night, all the doors were open and banging. The nun had disappeared but our glasses were on the table, and the traces of the orgy were still visible. The young nun – I still don't know her name, today – had placed the packet of laundry on a sideboard, but forgotten to take the dirty laundry away with her, which greatly surprised Teresa when she came back the following morning. Apart from that I have no idea what happened. The regular routine appears to have been re-established, and the laundry is collected and returned by two nuns of venerable age. All the same, I would be curious to know whether the young nun with the reddened hands remembers anything of what took place, and why it was that she came alone that day, when I was alone, too . . .'

Always slightly dishevelled, slightly old-fashioned, very much the libertine and wonderfully dandified, dear Max tells me half-a-dozen tall tales and astonishing anecdotes, until our memories lead us back to our hiding places of old, between the great trunks laid down in his father's sawmill warehouse. With the bitter, secret poetry of childhood, I find again the smell of bark, of sap, almost like ink, which is not the smell of forests, but of the agony of trees, the odour of coffins. The odour of transgression, too, because the warehouse was off limits to us and our games were only half-innocent. I remember the crumbling Savoy biscuits. The taste of coloured crayons. I remember how in Max's house, and mine, the same dim light filtered through the garden shutters, the same lime-washed, waxed floors creaked underfoot, the same fine cotton curtains draped our childhood beds; it was a world of hoops and batons and sailor suits, of games in the gravel and leaves, of scraped knees and stones, but I do not remember ever telling how I laid an owl's skeleton to rest in the soil. The finest secrets are invariably those we do not share.

Max recounted the extraordinary adventure of the laundress nun, and knowing him as I do, I see no reason to doubt it. A parenthesis: the image of the nun flopping like a sack on the bidet awakens the memory of my uncle flopping like a sack, himself, supported by his two sons. It may even, by twisting paths, suggest Sarpedon borne along by Hypnos and Thanatos, since that picture is readily associated with the circumstances of my uncle's demise, though to say so seems like sacrilege.

PIERRE SENGES
from *Geometry in the Dust*

translated from the French by Jacob Siefring

Much in the style of Montesquieu's Persian Letters, *Pierre Senges'* Geometry in the Dust *views the features of the modern city through foreign eyes. The book's narrator, a Bedouin counselor, has been entrusted with a difficult task: to describe the city to 'someone who has always only ever known sand and its forms through the cycle of seasons'. The counselor's earnest descriptions, which are his letters addressed home to his king, will serve as blueprints, permitting them to erect a city all of their own making, a monument to their glory.*

The four chapters published here – 2, 12, 13 and 14 – describe the unique difficulty of the counselor's task, the rites taking place in the city's secular temples, its dead-ends and cul-de-sacs, and the bittersweet necessity of leaving that city, once and for all.

Géométrie dans la poussière was published by Éditions Verticales in 2004 with twenty-six black-and-white drawings by Killoffer. It was the first and only title in a new series entitled, one wonders how such books find their way into readers' hands. *Indeed. We are grateful to the book's publisher for permission to reproduce several of those images alongside our selection of the text.*

– J.S.

How does one form an idea of the city, when all one has seen of it are tiny pieces of it brought back in trunks from voyages? How to describe a metropolis to someone who has always only ever known sand and its forms through the cycle of seasons? How to speak of snow to a Moor, or of cannibalism to a vegetarian Jesuit? He who, in the year 180 of the Hegira, wanted to tell Harun al-Rashid's eunuchs about sexual intercourse ended up getting lost in his own metaphors (no one ever saw him come back out, but one consoles oneself for his absence with a collection of paraphrases found at the site where he vanished). I imagine that, since my departure, you have forced yourself to roll up our sketches inside each other, and that you've read the works of Ibn Battuta over once again. But if you wish to imagine the city, I would sooner advise you go to the ancient, long-abandoned port of Antioch and admire the breaking of the waves there, or instead measure their angles without letting yourself be distracted by the waters; you can discover contentment in the palm of your hand, since there, as in the city, the idea of fate finds itself superimposed on the idea of lines, and every line supposes a direction to take, adventures to be had, the principle of fatality neighboring the principle of chance, neither set free nor enslaved by it; on the night of Eid al-Adha you will be able to look on with approval as a lamb carcass is flayed, and especially on the insertion of knife between skin and bone, as you hope that this mélange of savoir-faire, of virtuosity, of cruelty, of mathematics and of cadaver (the living creature, in the planner's hands) will not unjustly call to mind the city as it presents itself to my eyes: that is one way, among other ways, of introducing algebra into nature. (You can also, without saying so much as a word, watch two wrestlers, while keeping about your person that taciturn attitude sovereigns have before they pronounce judgment, and then attentively watch as the two opponents, finding their strengths to be equal and maybe the true balance of their artificially inculcated rancor, lock their two bodies in a posture that seems as though it would last forever, a posture which is no longer that of conflict, but one of harmony, and, as nothing else moves, of a love of which we were previously unaware.) You can wait

for nightfall to look on the stars, spending your hours that way, alternately forgetting and then recalling the various constellations, their names and shapes, because in that alternation more than in order itself you will receive the impression one has of the city on certain evenings; you can find contentment inspecting obscurity in all its forms, without so much as hoping to find in them an exact description of the city, you will be able to teach yourself how to distinguish between various shades of black, and to draw from that difference an epithet that can be applied to the city (as difficult to capture as a mosquito with one's eyes closed). If that does not work, you will rip apart a musical instrument, the soundboard of a lute; you will observe of what material its soul is formed: two or three pieces of wood oriented according to principles beyond our grasp; you will be able to observe a lock-and-key mechanism, able to learn the names of things at the same time as the things themselves (grooves, teeth). To men who have only ever known the desert and its dawns, its bivouacs, the little tufts of its oily plants and the obstinacy of the herds, Hafez advises (unhelpfully perhaps) to shoot an arrow straight ahead of oneself while reciting random pages from an encyclopedia (he had the *Sydrac* in mind, composed at Toledo).

To describe a jellyfish to someone who has never seen one: that would be like describing a drop of milk dropped into a glass of water. But to convey what a jellyfish is to someone who has knowledge of neither jellyfish nor milk drop? That would amount to a different order of challenge, or rather, another order of spiritual exercise. Addressing a desert prince, whosoever would describe the city (a generic city, all cities, this particular city) can invoke the metal shard (of the teapot), the bolt (of the safe), the rope lattice (of the tent); with his finger he can designate the patterns in the carpet, if he is cleverer than the ordinary man, he can make an indirect allusion to oiled parchment, rolled up into an amulet and wrapped in a page from a holy book – but all these measures will be in vain and mediocre, the descriptions will be lost in allegories, the proximity of the desert's forces to these speeches will be such that sand will cover them, and the idea of flat surfaces prevail over the complicated recesses of the city. I for my part would only be able to tell you this: nothing differentiates a city from the reflections of that city observed (perceived) in a mirror's shattered surface. It's the same thing, really, it's just as it looks: a city comprised of sections of wall, angles of roof, pieces of glass or zinc, mosaics, crossties, vehicles flying past, of course mirrors too, which seem to have, in advance as it were, been born of a broken mirror's reflections – or the mirror's actual division (little does it matter anyways, what explanations are offered for these piecemeal divisions: as the story goes, there were Vandals, uprisings, youths wielding slingshots, long-smoldering revolts, traffic accidents, insurance frauds, hold-ups: all like so many stars gleaming in the shop windows). To have a fragmentary vision of the city is not the proof of our impotence, it's the best that we can do, we who have dreamed for so long of being jolted by streetcars and lampposts.

*

Your city will be a place of profound dignity and detachment; the usual forms of modesty and reserve will be on display there, excessive sometimes, sometimes offset by crises of affectivity (you will see to it that ambulating preachers declaim in a loud voice their love for the entire human race, and of wine – alternately, it will be the job of others, though in the same grime-encrusted circumstances, to occupy themselves with maledictions: thus every city must accommodate one or two millenarians, in shirt-sleeves, in gabardines, not always clean-shaven): your city, like the one I am studying, will not be a place where strangers embrace one another spontaneously, except in times of celebration or affliction. Nevertheless, you should maintain places where confidences are allowed, and certain forms of tenderness between natives and non-natives permitted. I do not mean to say that fornication should be tolerated, but that certain barriers of modesty or prudence should be dropped there, following a precise gradation, all the while respecting rituals as sensitive as morning glories to the flux of the day's hours until nightfall. The confessional in the temples is a respectable institution, but it is no longer fashionable, and it quickly becomes uncomfortable given that whoever frequents it must remain upright on a stiff board and breathe in through holes: the box in which we are cloistered also has the disadvantage of being narrow, automatically prohibiting the spirit of amity and concord or even of embrace that accompanies confidences – and yet confidences are in fact exchanged, given in return for a sort of weary, professional magnanimity. Allow me this advice, as your faithful minister: I would not advise you to construct this sort of *mashrabiya*-like furniture in the temples of your city (this type of confessional has already disappeared anyways, or it almost has, owing, I think, to the bull of a Roman bishop, which soon reached most of the capitals of the Christian world). I would instead advise you to build, in lieu of churches, though taking inspiration from them, places that are vaster and less austere, secular down to their every minute detail, and comfortable too, the stalls being lined with moleskin and even stuffed with synthetic foam more often than not – comfortable also because music may be heard there, crooners' music and ritornellos (the *lacrimosa* probably, in a profane rendition accompanied by a brass section), and because cold beverages are served on-site. In the smoke of many sticks of incense pursed between the lips, under the authority of a master of ceremonies in black and white behind his altar, possessed of an archdeacon's petrified neutrality except if (and when) things come to blows, the penitents deliver themselves over to confidence, pretending to read their memories (their venial sins) in the bottoms of their liquor glasses. Certain of them, seated close to the altar and resting their elbows in accordance with the protocol, are great purveyors of confidences: if they find an ear, they address themselves to it without much in the way of manners directly after a few introductory formulae, unless they have the dignified and modest habit of addressing their remarks to themselves: there being not the least narcissism in that confession to

Priests? There are a great number of them in the city, but they may nevertheless be found less numerous than the defrocked priests of every observance: the disillusioned of the Society of Jesus, the orphans of the City of the Sun, and those who stopped believing (yesterday, in fact) in utopian societies.

oneself, nor the least autoeroticism; these confidants lavish on themselves the precise, minuscule amount of attention they consider their due, no more. What the architect prince must also know: these grand penitents not only specialize in confidences, they also become the petty colporteurs of a collective knowledge which is vital to the city's proper functioning: they are colporteurs with short-term memories, the guardians of proverbial wisdom, the guarantors of received ideas, archivists of the *a priori* (in the same way that the Minister of Justice will be your Keeper of the Seals); they are depositaries of rumor and the fresh scoop; sometimes they are receivers of very old stories, anecdotes linked in an arbitrary or amusing way to the great moments of the universal chronicle; they are also custodians of secrets that no longer have anything to do with anyone or anything, since they are obsolete. Their duty is to transmit the charades and silly stories while deforming them as little as possible; through a surfeit of zeal they secure the rights to jokes invented aeons ago. The most audacious among them are pioneers when it comes to social theories: in the unfolding of an utterance that is as frail as it is rancorous can be fleetingly glimpsed the outlines of whole philosophies; certain among them have enough aplomb to pronounce syllogisms (always impressive) and invent axioms based on other axioms, keeping the corollaries to themselves, not saying a word as they hermetically withhold grave and savant conclusions, with a taciturn, slightly stupefied air (or mournful: see how preoccupied they are). They do not keep silent: they resolve to be silent, but with reservations, which is not quite the same thing: for the whole assembly is informed of their silence.

You should thus construct a vast confessional, starkly illumined except for a few zones of shadow (in amber tones), outfitted with curves inspired by Turkish harems (banquettes, coat racks, elbow rests, foam of hot chocolate); a confessional where the aspergillum will be filled with the alcohol of fermented prunes, and where the penitents will rush forth like the damned as represented by Paul van Limburg, at the very bottom of Hell, on its ground floor, under the devil's foot. There, you must know how to drink to the dregs to merit a friendship that is with every sip the more frank and true; you must know how to grip a peanut between two fingers; you must also learn to admire the simplicity of a fried egg. Rhapsodies will be heard there: for want of professional musicians (oud, tambourines), some savants devised ingenious music boxes, probably taking inspiration from the designs of al-Jazari: imagine a mill decked out like a Berber bride. It was in such places, frequented by faithful players, that I caught wind of this hypothesis: all the parlor games existing the world over might have as their sole raison-d'être the desire to form an exact idea of the city – that is why I am attaching a set of playing cards to this report by means of a length of flax: in order to convince you that the city is but a mélange of strip poker, patience and *belote*.

A peanut between two fingers: according to calculations verified by experience, observers count about as many men in the city as peanuts in the city's bowls; moreover, men regularly take hold of peanuts, by the fistful or one after the other, in the vain hope of mastering unity, great sums, the present moment, or even that false eternity born of accumulation. As I became aware of its qualitative and quantitative

importance in every domain of a city's life, I forced myself to study the peanut in greater detail, and thence to find its precise definition (to do it perfect justice while situating it in the context of a vast agglomeration). I believe I can now say: the peanut is one of the most frustrating forms of the present moment. Otherwise put: the common, domestic, roasted and salted peanut is to the universe of beings as the second is to the temporal universe: its constitutive unity, however deceptive due to its elusive nature, impalpable, lacking in thickness yet not intangible, just as soon here as vanished, far too short for the senses, for consciousness, or for all the combined energies of mind and body to form a definitive opinion of it, or simply perceive it in its entirety. Neither peanut nor second see themselves, they exist either by the illusion of a capture refuted by the facts, either *in absentia*, by the very fact of their disappearance, or as an arbitrary construction of spirit: 1/86184 of the sidereal day for the second, a humble fraction of a ten-millionth of a quarter of the terrestrial meridian for the peanut. The salted peanut, a unit of space? Perhaps; and if the poet Ramón de Castile were brought back for a visit to this country of interminable *apéritifs*, he would see in the peanut, or the fistful of peanuts, the equivalent of Hop o' my Thumb's pebbles, tracing a direct path, unit by unit, from one form of thirst to the next.

*

For me, a most glaring form of failure (upon first sight), a defeat that must be compared to the sorry return of the empty-handed mujahideen (not the mujahideen, but some stumps of the mujahideen, and stumps of cavalry): when, for the first time in this city that serves as our model, I collided with the end of a cul-de-sac, when I admitted with my nose, then with my forehead, the presence of a wall without an opening, I thought that the impasse was a single mistake, a forgivable error in an otherwise perfect city. Since the city is a rigorous mathematics inhabited by scores of people, it could not contain the least fault, or the eyes of accountants and geometers would have noticed the discrepancy: such a cul-de-sac could only be an anomaly then, a dash of teratology in an otherwise healthy body, wisely tolerated for reasons of local hygiene, prudence, or because some small imperfection is necessary to ensure (this is well known) the cohesion of the whole.

To find an explanation for cul-de-sacs: perhaps they exist for reasons of humility, the cul-de-sac being a form of incompleteness and a symbol corresponding to the city-dwellers' imperfection, as opposed to the omnipresence and omniscience of God; it might serve in the interests of superstition, since cities can have recourse to cul-de-sacs in order to entrap demons, driving them in and blocking their exit by means of pistols and torches; it could be a work of art, a way to exploit litotes and the unsaid, the cul-de-sac would then be the equivalent of a sonnet consisting of a single line of verse with a single foot, or instead an elegy dedicated to the brevity of life, to a deceased fiancée perhaps; or an effect of a particularly acute form of melancholy that would have overcome the roadworkers when it came time to lay down the roads, in which case the furthest extremity of the cul-de-sac, that muzzled horizon where someone lives against all odds, with abandon, would be tantamount to a disarming *what's the use?*; it could be a matter of farce, insofar as farces rely on twists and involve sabotage and trompe-l'œil effects, stage props, like the dagger with a retracting blade, and painted backdrops; it might correspond to the designs of a young architect who wearied of aligning triumphal thoroughfares and was glad to lodge for just himself and a handful of his friends, in the heart of a city never caught off guard, a street that never lets out, a street in which – of this he can be sure – no one will ever come to parade; it could be a matter of a prince's caprice, a prince of your ilk: he would have broken a boulevard clean off in order to sow grass at its extremity, just as certain kings slice off heads and others reroute rivers; it could be the result of a superficial error in perspective, disguised as a square; it might correspond to an act of fraud, or a sudden bankruptcy.

Many strolls I took, and a great many impasses did I find: to come upon a first cul-de-sac was a surprise for me, coming upon a second led to feelings of confusion and helplessness, the third struck me as an outright deception, and so on subsequently, until ire was attained (the seventeenth cul-de-sac), scorn (the twenty-sixth and twenty-seventh cul-de-sacs), indifference (somewhere around the fortieth), and serenity (the one hundred-and-ninth cul-de-sac, the very last: I believe I have counted them all, I think I made a U-turn at the bottom of every one). But I soon had to eat my hat (my turban): the impasse in the city is no anomaly, no miscalculation, it is not some humiliating pig's tail in the form of a corkscrew: for the excessively high number of cul-de-sacs in the city requires us to revise our every judgment. With regard to their impasses, the locals here have abandoned their feelings of shame, embarrassment and frustration; while they were taking certain liberties with modesty, including shortening their skirts, and giving notice to their patron saints, they learned to conquer their natural disgust, and thus came to know the barren beauty of lanes without exits. They found there a colorless charm, which is all to their credit. They knew how to put these isolated locations to good use, and how to surreptitiously organize romantic rendezvous and Juliette-on-the-balcony scenes on certain summer days. Soon they no longer felt offended by a road leading nowhere, sufficient unto itself, ironic but in a most simple way; they also understood that the impasse has the tremendous advantage of putting an end (it was so simple) to the building of roads, which is a principle without end, a form of unending growth that would sooner or later bring on the city's collapse, through its occupation of the whole territory. With the taboo lifted, my dear prince of the sand, you are within your rights to welcome this piece of information with the relief felt at the absolution of all one's sins, or at the pardon granted to a man formerly condemned to die: from now on you will be able to partake of this new game, to add a chosen number of cul-de-sacs to your city, facetious like Shakespeare's Puck – I for my part would like there to be ninety-nine of them, but you are the sole master.

*

Being masters of the city means we must also consider the moment when we will have to leave it behind. In other words, it means we must devise fugue forms compatible with all we have learned of the modern metropolis (without betraying our oriental land: for it is the source of our charm, as well as of our terracotta tint). From where I stand in this model city, this city that I know perfectly from having measured it with a ruler (but in which I still cut the figure of a foreigner: a sorry silhouette with my burnoose, my nose like a vulture's beak), I too am preparing to leave. I will leave the city because there are many ways of doing so, and because among all those possibilities, I perhaps have a chance to form yet another idea of the city – by quitting it, that is. Idle tales have been told (worse than idle, pedagogical, rather) of Gomorrah, or Sodom, from which you would think, without really believing it, that to look back at a city after leaving it for good amounts to apprehending it in an impartial, neutral way (the vision of an architect, but also of Last Judgment). It seems probable that the best sketches are those made from a distance; I don't mean by casting a glance of scorn over one's shoulder, but by mixing nostalgia and the panoramic view (a view from a neighboring hill), by combining surveyor's data, held under the elbow, with memories made all the more vivid by the voluntary exile's firm resolve. For a geometer like myself who takes down his measurements on tablets according to the instructions laid out in *The Book of Rare Things in the Art of Calculation*, to pack one's bags doesn't mean saying grandiloquent goodbyes, but an end to the process of measurement: because our professional conscience, known also as scruples, demands that we follow a single straight line or two parallel lines out past the city's official limits, to see whether they have not been damaged (a pretext, of course: were I kicked out by force, I would say I was going off to the other side of the unknown territories to roll out my tape measure; that way would I keep my chin up).

One of our own proverbs states the following: the theorem of Thales is used to measure surfaces, but dust has a method unto itself.

(To quit the city that served as our model: what could be more

Pierre Senges

normal than that? My mission presupposed that I would return to my country. Except that this departure will be my first, and I will probably need to procure some precursors in this regard, in order to follow their examples, or to draw lessons from their experiences: these would help to reassure me that I am not some maladroit pioneer. I will try hard to remind myself how Abu Abdallah fled Granada, torn between ceremonial dignity and the tact of a feral dog; how Pope Clement left Rome, taking with him all the Vatican's crockery, and the Savior's authentic prepuce too; and how Frederick II left Jerusalem after becoming its king; how Shakespeare left London while pretending to sweep the messy aftermath of Hamlet's adventures under the rug; and, lastly, how the infidel Casanova, like a hoofer on a hot tin roof, sniveling and philosophizing, managed to escape Venice.)

But it's not just to quit the city that served me as model – it's also to leave behind the city that we will have at last constructed. To leave our home? Perhaps, if by then your city-dwelling subjects have elected to chase us off, if we show ourselves to be greedy and arrogant, for instance, unjust in the court of justice, and overgenerous on the stock exchange, irresponsible every which way, and if you estimate that your majesty, after having taken your seat on the throne, requires still more distance to perfect itself – you will be driven out of your own city if, finding the idea of a French leavetaking too scandalous, you would prefer that your own people collectively expel you in a rite that combines insurrection and saturnalia, the peasant's revolt and official festivities: your people will expatriate you the better to lose sight of you, and the better to situate you metaphorically atop Mount Olympus alongside the demigods (some centuries later, devotion and resentment will become as one).

That would be only one possibility among others: but we will not be chased out if we see to it that the ramparts are made impregnable to a prince and his minister, each burdened with a valise. We will be happy just to die a modest death, at such-and-such a fixed place in your capital, after a long, heady agony in the decadent style (a loose, indolent style, steeped in a serenity that no one would try to define exactly, for fear that it might be lost – an end of a reign containing the first hints of intrigue, like the germs of a future still to come). We won't play chess anymore, we will station ourselves on either side of a chessboard, not lifting so much as a pinky, nor the bishop, nor the rook – and all of your secretaries will be under strict orders not to disturb us for however long the period of our immobility should last. Every now and then, to give ourselves the appearance of working, we will take out the plans for our city again, and the numerous ink sketches I brought back from that city; we will be like Nero and Harun al-Rashid, who disguised themselves as bread-men to slip unrecognized into the girls' quarters; by night we will go off to verify our documentation, and we will take pains to reconstruct the most minute details, those that seem to cry out with truth – (all up and down each street: as deft as stray kids ringing doorbells). A most peaceful way to await our final hour – and once everything has been taken care of, we will spend our afternoons finalizing our plans for a hypogeum, with two headstones (cut from the gray-yellow marble of Aleppo – the city of Sayf al-Dawla).

RED SQUIRREL

QUALITY CONTEMPORARY POETRY AND FICTION

Red Squirrel Press

is a completely independent publisher printing pamphlets, full collections, and themed anthologies. It showcases young poets such as Claire Askew and Andrew McMillan, as well as more established names like James Kirkup, William Bedford and Pippa Little. Visit the website for news, details of competitions, submission guidelines, and to browse and buy.

e: editor@redsquirrelpress.com
www.redsquirrelpress.com

Contributors

Sophie Lewis, editor of this issue of *Sonofabook*, is senior editor at And Other Stories press, where she has edited fiction by Deborah Levy, Juan Pablo Villalobos and Oleg Pavlov, among others. She also translates from French and Portuguese. She has translated works by Stendhal, Jules Verne, Marcel Aymé, Violette Leduc, Emmanuelle Pagano and João Gilberto Noll. In 2015 she moved back to London after nearly five years in Rio de Janeiro.

*

Born Kurdish Syrian in 1951, in 1970 **Salim Barakat** went to study literature in Damascus and then in Beirut, where he stayed until 1982, publishing five volumes of poetry, two novels, a diary and two volumes of autobiography. By 1999, when he moved to Sweden, he had published his tenth book of poetry and a further seven novels. Barakat's early poetry was revolutionary for its time. He is also known for innovative prose which includes elements of magical realism.

Dan Bellm is a poet and translator living in Berkeley, California. His latest book, *Practice*, won the 2009 California Book Award in Poetry. His translation of Pierre Reverdy's *Song of the Dead* (1948) will appear from Black Square Editions/Brooklyn Rail in 2016. He teaches literary translation and poetry at Antioch University, Los Angeles.

Uilleam Blacker is Lecturer in Comparative East European Culture at the School of Slavonic and East European Studies, University College London. He has written widely on Ukrainian, Polish and Russian literature and culture, and has translated the work of several contemporary Ukrainian writers. His translations have appeared in Words Without Borders and the Dalkey Archive *Best European Fiction* series, as well as in individual publications.

Luke Carman is the author of *An Elegant Young Man* (Giramondo, 2013), which was recently awarded a NSW Premier's Literary Award and shortlisted for the ALS Gold Medal. In 2014 he was named a *Sydney Morning Herald* Best Young Novelist. He is the Associate Director of SWEATSHOP.

Australian-born **Alison Entrekin** translates novels, short stories, poetry and children's books from Portuguese. Her translations include *City of God* by Paulo Lins, *The Eternal Son* by Cristovão Tezza, *Near to the Wild Heart* by Clarice Lispector, *Budapest* by Chico Buarque and *Crow Blue* by Adriana Lisboa.

Lorna Scott Fox is a translator, editor and journalist. She lived in Mexico in the '80s and '90s (publishing an early report on the 1994 Zapatista uprising in the *London Review of Books*), then moved to Spain, and is now based in London. Her most recent translations are, from French, *Teresa, My Love*, by Julia Kristeva (Columbia University Press, 2014), and from Spanish, *Politics in a Time of Crisis*, by Pablo Iglesias (Verso, 2015).

Julián Herbert (b. 1971, Acapulco, Mexico) is a poet, novelist, musician and performance artist. He has published six volumes of poetry, two short story collections and three novels. His playful, experimental, often melancholic writing, steeped in high and low culture, has won national and international awards, and been translated into several languages. However, no complete work has yet appeared in English.

Jennifer Higgins is a translator, editor and teacher. She has translated for Gallic Books, among others. Her most recent project has been co-translating *Nouons-nous*, a collection of French micro stories by Emmanuelle Pagano, with Sophie Lewis. This will be published by And Other Stories in 2016.

Sawad Hussain is an Arabic translator and litterateur. She holds a MA in Modern Arabic Literature from SOAS. She is passionate about all things related to Arab culture, history and literature. She is currently translating a Jordanian sci-fi novel out for release in early 2017.

Louise Rogers Lalaurie has translated five novels, numerous short stories and over thirty works of literary non-fiction (art and heritage, travel, memoir). Her translation of *Murder Most Serene* by Gabrielle Wittkop won a French Voices award in 2013, and is published by Wakefield Press (2015). She is an occasional blogger at *Astonishing travellers: translations from France* (http://louiserogers.wordpress.com).

Adriana Lisboa was born in Rio de Janeiro. Her debut novel *Symphony in White* won the José Saramago Prize and *Crow Blue* was voted one of the best books published in 2013 by *The Independent*. Her novels, poetry and short stories have been published in eighteen countries.

Born in September 1969, **Emmanuelle Pagano** has published twelve books, including novels, novellas, and collections of short stories and fragments, and many texts in magazines and other collections. Resident writer at the Villa Médicis in 2013-2014, winner of the European Union Prize for Literature in 2009, her books have been translated into a dozen languages. Often collaborating with artists from other disciplines (dance, cinema, photography, illustration, music), she lives and works in the plains of the Ardèche.

Taras Prokhasko was born in 1968 in Ivano-Frankivsk in western Ukraine. He chose to study to be a botanist despite his love for language and literature because he 'couldn't imagine himself as a Soviet writer'. Prokhasko did start to write, however, and in the late 1990s and early 2000s was at the heart of the so-called 'Stanislav phenomenon' (after the old name for Ivano-Frankivsk, Stanislaviv), an explosion of creative energy that centred on his native city and produced some of contemporary Ukraine's best young writers. After a varied career as a botanist, barman, radio presenter and political activist, he is now best known as a journalist and prose writer, and is the author of several books of fiction and essays and two children's books, written together with Mariana Prokhasko. In 2007 he was awarded the Joseph Conrad Literary Prize. His works have appeared in translation in Polish, German, Russian and English.

M Lynx Qualey edits the website 'Arabic Literature (in English)', found at www.arablit.org.

Pierre Reverdy (1889–1960), hailed by André Breton as 'the greatest poet of the time', championed many other poets and painters through his groundbreaking journal Nord-Sud, founded in 1917 with Max Jacob and Guillaume Apollinaire. He was also closely associated with Pablo Picasso, Henri Matisse, Georges Braque and Juan Gris, each of whom illustrated one or more of his books. Yet after living at the centre of French poetry and culture for some fifteen years, Reverdy withdrew from it almost completely in 1926, leaving Paris for the northern village of Solesmes, but continuing to write and to live what he called a 'quasi-monastic life'.

Pierre Senges is the author of fourteen books and over sixty plays for radio. His original fictions often unfold in the margins of other texts as inversions, variations, and commentaries on existing texts and historical figures. He is the recipient of prizes for *Veuves au maquillage* (2000), *Ruines-de-Rome* (2002), and his radio work. His most recent work, *Achab (séquelles)*, was awarded the Prix Wepler in 2015. At present only one of his books is available for purchase in English translation: *The Adventures of Percival: A Phylogenetic Tale* (Dis Voir, 2009).

Jacob Siefring is a Canadian-American translator. His translations of the short writings of Pierre Senges have appeared in *Gorse Journal*, *The White Review*, *Hyperion*, *The Collagist*, *3:AM Magazine*, *Numéro Cinq Magazine*, and elsewhere. His translation of *The Major Refutation* by Pierre Senges is forthcoming from Contra Mundum Press in 2016.

Gabrielle Wittkop was born in Nantes in 1920. She taught herself to read by the age of four – 'I got the feeling of absolute power' – and was schooled at home before leaving for Paris where she met and married the homosexual Nazi deserter, Justus Wittkop, in a union 'of friendship and affection'. Wittkop has a keen fan base in France and her adopted country, Germany. Self-styled female heir to de Sade, Wittkop is widely translated, although the only English translations to date are a 2011 Canadian edition of *The Necrophiliac*, translated by Don Pabst, and *Murder Most Serene* (2015) translated by Louise Rogers Lalaurie. Wittkop took her own life aged 81, declaring that she intended to die as she had lived, 'a free man'.

With dreams of reforming and perfecting the universe, Argentine artist **Xul Solar** invented two languages, a spiritual form of chess and a modified piano, and painted works based on his own blend of cosmic mysticism. After a spell in Europe, in l924 he returned to Buenos Aires, the imaginary antipodes of the North, and joined the Southern Avant Garde. There, in his own house, he created his Pan-Klub, and his work entered the imagination of Borges, Macedonio Fernández, Roberto Arlt, Leopoldo Marechal, Julio Cortázar, and countless young poets later gathered around the magazine *Xul* in the 1980s.

Booksellers to the stars, the triangle and a couple of squares. Officially, The Best Shop in Crystal Palace - *Time Out* London Local Awards 2014

50 Westow St, London SE19 3AF
booksellercrow.co.uk

A B the Albion BEatNik bookstore

34 Walton St, Oxford OX2 6AA
albionbeatnikbookshop@gmail.com

BOOKWORMS are always reading books, or are the larvae of various * insects, moths and beetles that live in and feed upon the pages of books.

[* *No single species can properly be called the bookworm*]

Central heating, the manufacturing materials of modern books, the poor state of the English language as is writ today, but chiefly the prevailing attention span of gnats, have curtailed their medieval activities.

BE MEDIEVAL
DO CHIVALROUS : READ A BOOK

looking glass /books

books & coffee & food & events

7 days a week 8.30 a.m. till late

36 Simpson Loan, Quartermile, Edinburgh EH3 9GG

0131 229 2902
www.lookingglassbooks.com
@lookingglassbks

THE WOODSTOCK BOOKSHOP

23 Oxford Street, Woodstock,
OX20 1TH
www.woodstockbookshop.co.uk
info@woodstockbookshop.co.uk

JOIN THE POETRY SOCIETY

Membership of the Poetry Society helps poets and poetry thrive

If you love poetry, we'd love to have you as a member. With our key publications, *The Poetry Review* and *Poetry News*, competitions, events, promotions and expert advice, we'll put you at the heart of what's happening in contemporary poetry.

Annual membership of the Poetry Society includes four issues of *The Poetry Review* and *Poetry News*, poetry competitions, special offers, discounts, poetry groups near you, our monthly ebulletins – and much, much more...

Poetry Society membership
INC. THE POETRY REVIEW

UK from £42 • Europe from £52
Rest of the world from £57
Concessions available

For details, contact membership@poetrysociety.org.uk • +44 (0)20 7420 9881

Subscribe to The Poetry Review

Be sure you don't miss out on the next exciting issue of *The Poetry Review* – take out your annual subscription today.

The Poetry Review (4 issues pa)
UK £34 • Europe £44 • RoW £49

THE POETRY SOCIETY

www.poetrysociety.org.uk